THE ONE WORLD TAROT:
ASTROLOGY, TAROT, AND
THE NEW AGE

By Crystal Love

Illustrated by Michael Hobbs

U.S. GAMES SYSTEMS, INC.

First Edition

10 9 8 7 6 5 4 3 2 1

Printed in Canada

U.S. GAMES SYSTEMS, INC.
179 Ludlow Street
Stamford, CT 06902 USA
www.usgamesinc.com

This knowledge is the king of education, the most secret of all secrets. It is the purest knowledge, and it gives direct perception of the self by realization.

—BHAGAVAD-GITA

ACKNOWLEDGMENTS

Firstly, I would like to acknowledge the initial origina-
tor of the tarot cards, that unknown person or persons
who envisioned the encapsulation of arcane astrological
knowledge into simple pictorial form. It has been handed
down to us through the unknown and untold generations, and survives intact to this day. This is a credit to
whomsoever originated them.

I would also like to thank the occultist Eliphas Levi
who, although has long since passed, was pivotal in the
conception and design of this deck by providing me with
the correct astrological correlations for the tarot, without
which, this deck would and could not be what it is today.
He never got around to designing a deck based on those
allocations. If he could see The One World Tarot, I hope
he would approve.

My heartfelt thanks must be expressed to Stuart
Kaplan at U.S. Games Systems, Inc., for having the faith
to take on The One World deck and enabling it to finally
come to fruition. I would also like to thank everyone else
at U.S. Games Systems for their enthusiasm and contribu-
tion to this project—especially Bobbie, Elizabeth, and
AnnMarie.

My extra special thanks and acknowledgments to
artist Michael Hobbs who—despite his own pressing work
commitments—devoted so much of his free time to trans-
late my original designs into the final digital artwork, and

who has added so much with his additional interpretations and designs. His hard work, his patience, and his encouragement were invaluable. This deck could not have come into being as it is, without him.

Lastly, I want to recognize the wonderful work of all the millions of tarot readers around the world, as well as their clients who—together—keep this ancient spiritual art alive.

THE ONE WORLD TAROT:
ASTROLOGY, TAROT, AND THE NEW AGE

Contents

INTRODUCTION

Rainbows, clouds, and dreams all exist nebulously in a fleeting moment of time. Their fragile existence is but brief. There is no solidity or form that we can grasp, hold onto, save, or keep. They are temporary additions to the kaleidoscopes of our lives, and to the backdrop of our individual dreams and dramas. The ethereal nature of creation is symbolized in their existence, and our deepest consciousness craves to understand their mystical and mysterious forms.

And so it is, that our lives—fleeting and fragile as any cloud—are played out against a shifting stage, the backdrop of reality no more real or solid than a dream. Again and again we look for stability in a world of whispering change, and yet truly, we find none. Nor can we—for it is the nature of creation to change and never to remain stationary.

But even change has a strange order to it. It comes and goes in its own time. Even in this world of fleeting forms and images, there are discernable cycles—like spring, summer, autumn, and winter—and it is to these cycles of creation that we are inexorably linked.

The seasons of our own lives too, are bound to these universal cycles of creation, and we rise and fall with them—like flotsam and jetsam on the tides of the oceans. We are not, and never have been, separate from the cosmos. We are part of it, and the currents of our fortunes are bound to these same universal rhythms and cycles.

Since the dawn of time, humanity has attempted to

decipher its fate by the study of these cycles, and it was to the heavens and the night sky—awash with stars glowing and glittering like diamonds—that we first turned to understand these cycles (as above, so below). Soon, the clockwork and predictable motion of the planets, the sun and the moon, confirmed that the cycles on earth were directly determined by planetary activity in our solar system and beyond. A detailed science soon emerged which charted and attempted to interpret these heavenly movements. This science became known as astrology.

According to astrologers, the ever-changing cycles of the cosmos—in particular the planetary activity around our own star, the sun—was somehow able to influence life on earth. The limited number of scenarios that can be played out on the stage of life, birth, and death seemed to be linked to these heavenly cycles.

In the cycles and currents of our own individual existence, there are only so many scenarios that can come into being. Happiness, sadness, richness, poverty, fame, anonymity, success, or failure—whatever our fate may be—are all linked, not only to our own actions, but also to universal cycles of increase and decrease, expansion and contraction.

By becoming aware of these cycles (and by predicting them in advance) we can learn how to harmonize with them, in the same way that predicting the tides of the oceans enables us to go with the flow, and not against it.

In the distant past, these archetypal astrological and universal energies were deciphered, and the science of astrology was born. Astrology remained on an ascendant star for many thousands of years before our modern culture arose, and it is only now that it is once again gaining respectability and popularity in our modern society.

At some unrecorded moment in history, the basic astrological energies which are said to orchestrate life on earth, the planets, the signs, and the three subdivisions of each individual sign, were symbolized in pictorial form, and the tarot cards that we know today were first born.

Hidden away in the simple symbolic images of the tarot cards, are deeper meanings than is first apparent to the eye. The tarot—more than anything—is an intuitive way of accessing the unconscious to determine the state of the cyclic growth of the individual.

The tarot is a mirror to our own unconscious. There is no magic, no fancy tricks necessary. The tarot is an a–z of our life's journeys, there for us to call upon when in need of guidance. Now acceptable in today's alternative culture and beyond, the tarot has—like the phoenix—risen from the ashes of intolerance and prejudice, to become the number one tool in today's world for instant feedback from the unconscious.

The intuitive self, the soul self, sees the images and recognizes the symbols at the level of the collective unconscious. We see our lives, our struggles, our hopes, our dreams, written clearly in front of us, so that we may call upon the unconscious to guide the conscious mind through the maze—the "maya," of life and illusion.

Since the first tarot deck was created many thousands

of years ago, many different visual interpretations have come into being. As we approach the Age of Aquarius, however, I believe it is time for the tarot to be refreshed and invigorated with color symbolism and modern design appropriate for the New Age, and at the same time firmly re-rooted to its correct astrological origins. The essence of the tarot remains untouched by time, and its wisdoms still reach us from its symbolic images.

Our paths in life are determined by karma, and our fate awaits us like an unknown guest. Only with awareness can we aspire to find our way in this vast and mysterious Universe we call home.

The tarot will guide us, inspire us, and inform us. The mysteries of the psyche will be illuminated when we consult its intuitive wisdom. Perhaps the tarot alone can share the secrets of our souls. In the tarot we may find knowledge and wisdom that will lead us back from matter to spirit—to overcome the ego, the separateness of self—and to realize that we are all integral parts of One World, both equal and interdependent.

With the tarot as guide and teacher, we can learn to grow and evolve, for I believe it is our ultimate destiny to reach enlightenment.

The symbolism in The One World Tarot deck is hopefully as pleasing, effective, and meaningful for you as it is for me.

I wish you much joy in working with your deck!

Crystal Love. London, July 2002.

PART ONE

THE ART OF DIVINATION

At the very heart of divination—whether tarot, I Ching, runes, astrology, tea leaves, pendulums, or a bag of old bones—is a necessity, a need to know, and an ability to interpret universal rhythms.

Many surviving ancient cultures still practice divination in rituals that have survived for thousands of years. But over the last five hundred years such practices were deemed heretical by the Church in Europe and America, and many were condemned to death for their beliefs.

The mystic arts were discredited by science and formal religion, surviving by necessity underground, as a subculture. They have not only remained intact over the ages, but in the last thirty years they have undergone a massive revival and popularity unsurpassed in our history. What was once considered "superstitious nonsense," "mumbo-jumbo," and "occult" is now finding its place in mainstream culture and has become part of our daily lives.

From the African tribal leader's ancient rituals to the modern parlors with tarot readers, rune readers, astrologers, psychics, mediums, and clairvoyants—one thing is for sure—we are now comfortably out of the "witchcraft closet." Right brain, mystical, and magical things are no longer considered "evil" and we are entering a New Age where all things spiritual and mystical, as long as they benefit society as a whole, are truly welcomed.

Now that we are on the cusp of the great age, the mysteries of the Piscean past will come under the scrutiny of Aquarian logic. Science and mysticism will find common terminology to define and express universal truths.

The most popular form of divination today is the tarot, a set of 78 printed visual images consisting of 22 Major Arcana, 40 Minor Arcana, and 16 Court cards. The tarot guides the user to understand hidden aspects of his or her psyche and to know future trends or events.

Divination may seem a spurious and haphazard business, in which the "fortune teller" is a charlatan reciting ambiguous predictions, having mastered the art of "cold readings." However, the tarot is a precise tool, a visual dictionary of the cosmic influences on Earth, directly linked to astrology and the cycles of life.

How does the tarot reflect and express the reality of our lives? How do its archetypal symbols consciously or unconsciously represent the potential of human life on Earth?

From ancient days, divination played a part in all cultures. The act of divination, "to divine, to know," is one of the oldest human rituals. As society developed, the rituals themselves, the tools with which we divine, became more sophisticated, as in the elaborately artistic images of modern tarot decks.

Our ancestors obviously had no such elaborate visual systems. The original forms of divining relied on materials that were available. Some of the oldest forms of divination relied on animal omens or oracles. In ancient times, birds were seen as messengers. The word auspice in Latin literally means "an observer of birds."

The existence of an intrinsic link between our environment and ourselves is a belief shared by many ancient peoples. Early humans understood that natural occurrences can be seen as signs, symbols, and omens that reflect events to come. For example, the drastic behavioral changes that animals show in the hours and days preceding natural disasters have long been recorded. In China, snakes have been observed awakening from hibernation in mid-winter, in the hours prior to an earthquake. The humble chicken and farmyard pigs of China are also carefully watched, as their behavior changes drastically prior to seismic activity.

Our immense technology cannot predict earthquakes, but the snake, chicken, and pig perhaps sense the earth's vibrations long before we do. Certain animals indeed have senses far beyond human capabilities. Dogs' range of hearing and smelling range is far greater than our own. Eagles have a range of vision nearly 70 times greater than ours. Creatures such as dolphins possess sensitive radar and communication systems.

Many old superstitions are watered down versions of intuitive wisdom based on the observation of animal behavior. An ancient rhyme about magpies says, "One is sorrow, two is mirth, three is a wedding, four is a birth."

Animals have also been used in less pleasant ways when divination was performed by examining the entrails or bones of sacrificial animals. The Turkana tribe in Kenya consulted their traditional healer for diagnosis of a health problem. The healer would request the patient to find a specific goat required for the healing ritual. The goat would then be sacrificed and its entrails examined to divine a cure.

Examinations of individual animal bones or of the symbolic pattern of bones thrown together on the ground were some of the earliest forms of divination practiced in Africa.

Perhaps one of the strangest forms of divining using animals was practiced by the North American Indians of southern California, the Tubatulabal. The ritual included a three-day fast, after which the one to "divine" would ingest seven balls of eagle's down, each containing five yellow ants reputed to have psychoactive properties. The "diviner" would then be violently shaken until the ants bit him, thus transmitting their chemical properties into his system. The diviner would fall into a stupor. When he awoke, he would recount his visions, and these visions would be used for guidance for tribal affairs (Rudgely, 2000).

As man became more intellectually and technologically adept and began to develop written language, primitive written oracles began to appear, simultaneously around the world.

An old North European form of divination was the Wiccan Oracle of the Talking Stones (Wise Stones). Similar in essence to rune stones, the stones were held in the left hand while the question was considered. The stones were then shaken and thrown to the ground. The nearest stone represented the present, and the furthest stone, the future. The simple symbols carved on the stones represented the possibilities inherent in life itself, and would be interpreted according to the question.

A far more complex form of divination was also developing among early civilizations. The Chinese, the ancient Indians, the Babylonians, the Egyptians, and the ancient Britons were coming to grips with perhaps the most sophisticated and complex divination system of all—astrology.

Since humankind first became autonomous and conscious of the world, we became aware of the fact that life moves in cycles, and that these cycles could be predicted precisely by the movements of the planets.

Nature's cycles—spring, summer, autumn, and winter, as well as night and day—are all determined by planetary movement. Fullness and want, life and death, all manifestation on Earth as we know it, according to astrology, is governed by the planetary bodies.

Astrology has been practiced by cultures dating back to Stonehenge and the Egyptian pyramids, and was considered one of the sacred sciences. In Renaissance Europe, astrology was not only acceptable, but also widely practiced. Queen Elizabeth I of England had a full-time personal astrologer, John Dee, who advised her on both personal matters and affairs of state. However, only fifty years after her death, Sir Isaac Newton developed his theories on the physical nature of the universe. His work led to the birth of modern physics and science, and heralded the decline in the philosophy and practice of magic and astrology.

Astrology is now regaining renewed credibility and popularity, to the point where millions of people consult their horoscopes in newspapers and magazines as an ongoing daily ritual.

Whichever form of symbolism is used to help divine, the very essence of divination is that we call upon our supernatural powers, our powers of intuition, and the power of the unconscious to interpret events. Each system of divination may vary in method, but the need to know is universal. We seek information unavailable to the conscious mind.

Divination can be seen to fall into three main categories:

• divination by altered states of consciousness—such as trance, dream, channeling, sometimes induced by psychoactive substances;

• divination by direct and conscious clairvoyance, clairaudient, and psychometric vibrations; and

• divination by external symbol systems—such as tarot, I Ching, runes, and astrology.

A common belief of many ancient religions and cultures is that certain persons are naturally gifted with the ability to divine, or to make contact with the "spirit worlds." The medicine man, witch doctor, shaman, or high priestess took on the role of medium between the spirit worlds—that which is invisible and unformed, and the material world, with all its attendant dreams and dramas.

But what makes us able, individually, to divine, to tune in?

The mind and the brain differ. This simple fact is vital to our understanding of how the supernatural and mystical operates in humankind. Mind is defined here as spirit or supreme consciousness, causative of all things, and omnipresent within them simultaneously. Mind, according to many ancient religions and philosophies, is not only omnipresent, but also interconnected. It is both a form of energy and a form of consciousness. Einstein's profound equation, $E = mc^2$, confirms that energy creates matter, and that matter itself is a by-product of energy. The materialized world is created from the energy, or spirit world. The spirit world already contains all the information about the form it is creating. In other words, future events already exist before they happen.

Mind is a nonphysical energy, or spirit, that pervades all living things, and is composed of a higher form of energy, which is known as spirit, prana, or ch'i—the divine in humans. The act of divination means to understand the divine plan, to know.

The brain is the physical organ through which the mind operates, connecting it to the physical body. Our brains do not, and cannot, perceive the divine, as the divine itself is nonphysical and beyond form. That which perceives the divine is the divine, nonphysical self, which is beyond space and time and which exists within us all.

Many examples of telepathic knowledge prove to us that we are all capable of thinking and perceiving beyond the space-time continuum as we know it. We are somehow able to know things beyond our senses and to see both backwards and forwards in time.

At the University of Edinburgh in Scotland, scientific research has been conducted in telepathy and ESP (extrasensory perception). In tests, randomly selected volunteers in fully controlled experiments have maintained a 45 percent success rate, defying all logic.

An even more intense study of telepathic powers with virtually 100 percent success rates was conducted for over two decades by a most unlikely source. This research was conducted by the United States government under the direction of the CIA (Central Intelligence Agency) and the top secret DIA (Defense Intelligence Agency) at Fort Meade, Maryland. The aim of the intelligence agencies was to gather information and penetrate intelligence targets, using "psychic spies" who could project their awareness anywhere in time/space. This was known as the Remote Viewing project.

Many of the subjects had a history of psychic experiences, including near death experiences and claims of contact with UFOs. One remote viewer had suddenly developed psychic abilities after a head injury received in combat. Other remote viewers had experience in imagery interpretations (reconnaissance) and had strong powers of visualization.

Later programs included experiments in psychokenesis, the ability to move objects with mind power alone. Several senior-ranking officers found themselves easily able to bend spoons, Uri Geller style. This was verified by reliable eyewitnesses.

Psychologist and author Dr. Keith Harary, a remote viewer himself between 1980 and 1982, said that he got his impressions through almost subliminal images and feelings, as though one part of the mind was trying to communicate with the other—feeling, smelling, and tasting perceptual parts of the experience. Another remote viewer said that it was as if he had a scanner and opened a channel to receive this data. A prominent member of the military personnel involved in the Remote Viewing program stated categorically, "We know there's something there. We can't explain it, but we know it works."

Although the Remote Viewing program was designed for military and espionage purposes in response to Russian research, the evidence accumulated during twenty years of research will go a long way to substantiate the paranormal.

All of us are capable of telepathic feats of one sort or another, enabling us to "pick up" invisible signals much like the animals of China do before earthquakes.

We all regularly have prophetic dreams, according to J.W. Dunne (2001). Having satisfied himself that he regularly dreamt of future events, Dunne wrote, "That the universe was, after all, really stretched out in time, and that the lopsided view we had of it—a view with the 'future' part unaccountably missing, cut off from the growing 'past' part by a traveling 'present moment'—was due to a purely mentally imposed barrier which existed only when we were awake, so that in reality the network stretched, not merely this way and that way in space, but also backwards and forward in time."

Dreams and visions have played an important part in many cultures. References to prophetic dreams abound in ancient scripture. Indeed the Old and New Testaments have over twenty accounts of dreams that offered divine guidance in the form of warnings and prophecies. Dreams have been used for prophecy and guidance as long as people have been dreaming, and many great historical and cultural events have been shaped by dreams.

Perhaps the most ironic of prophetic dreams occurred to a young corporal on a cold November night in the trenches of the First World War. He awoke from a terrible nightmare in which his bunker had been totally destroyed by enemy fire. As he rushed breathless into the cold night air from his terrible vision, the bunker was instantly hit by French artillery, killing all the occupants asleep inside. The name of that young corporal was Adolf Hitler (Dee, 1984).

The North American Indians recognized the value of their dreams and visions as a source of information. The

Huron and Iroquois held regular dream festivals that lasted days, or even weeks. During the festivals they would note, compare, and pool the information from their dreams and visions and use them for guiding tribal affairs.

That greatest of Native American warriors, Tatanka Yotanka, better known as Sitting Bull, a Teton Sioux of the Kupapa tribe, had many well-documented prophetic dreams and visions. His dream of the defeat of General Custer at the Battle of Little Big Horn is legendary.

To achieve an altered state for experiencing visions, Tatanka Yotanka underwent rituals that many people today would find beyond strength and endurance. The rituals included fasting and self-mutilation. At one Sun Dance, after three days of such rituals, Tatanka Yotanka had a vision in which he saw many white soldiers falling from their horses in the sky. From this he concluded that he would be victorious in his forthcoming battles, and so he was. However, his successes were insufficient to halt the path of history and he was the last of such great Native American warriors.

Crazy Horse, a young and daring brave of the Oglala Sioux, and a friend of Sitting Bull, believed that the everyday world is only a shadow of the "real" world. To get into the real world he said, he had to dream, and when he was in the real world matter seemed to dance or vibrate. In the real world his horse would seem to dance as if it were crazy and this is why he called himself Crazy Horse (Brown, 1991).

Dreams as the gateway to another dimension are now popularized by a combination of neo-Pagan subcultures, which embrace shamanistic practices and beliefs, and modern dream analysis pioneered by Freud and Jung. The question is, if we are capable of such psychic feats while sleeping, why are we not able to replicate easily these feats with the conscious mind?

The human brain is composed of two halves, known as the left brain and the right brain. They are connected by 300 million nerve fibers known as the corpus callosum. The left brain governs logical and analytical functions (active, male, yang), and the right brain governs intuitive and imaginative functions (receptive, female, yin). (The reverse is true for left-handed people.) The human brain, then, is like the yin-yang symbol itself, one half yin, one half yang. One half perceives the conscious world (matter), and the other half perceives the unconscious world (spirit).

Recent electromagnetic resonance photographs of the human brain, taken during controlled experiments at Yale University by researchers Bennett and Shaywitz, showed that men tend to use only the left part of the brain, whereas women used both halves of the brain simultaneously. Traditionally, women have been known to possess special psychic powers, a "sixth sense" or "women's intuition." No wonder then that a large percentage of New Age therapists, healers, astrologers, and counselors are women. Women's ability to tap into their right brains—emotions, sensitivity, and intuition—is legendary. That is not to say that men are any less capable of expressing or developing these abilities. As we approach the New Age, men will be encouraged to express their "feminine" side (right brain) and develop their sensitivity and supernatural powers.

In the process of divination, we must contact the right side of our brains, our unconscious, or the superconscious. The superconscious itself is connected to the whole universe and contains all information from the beginning to the end of time.

Many methods are employed to access the superconscious while in the process of divination. Meditation or relaxation serves to pacify the logical left brain. Ritualized, hypnotic singing, drumming, dancing, and chanting have served our ancestors for thousands of years as a means of inducing altered states of consciousness.

This works by altering brain rhythms and brain waves. There are four kinds of brain waves: alpha, beta, delta, and theta. Each produces a different frequency range of electrical activity. Delta is the slowest, giving a reading of 4 cycles per second. This slow wave is associated with deep sleep. The theta rhythm operates between 4 and 7 cycles per second and is associated with the dream state. The alpha rhythm gives a reading of 8 to 13 cycles per second and is associated with meditation and relaxation. The beta rhythm operates at 13 to 30 cycles per second and is found in the normal waking state.

Human beings are capable not only of generating these waves, but of receiving them. In the center of the forehead lies the pineal gland, known to us now as the "third eye" center. In our aquatic cousins, the dolphins, a magnetic sonar is located in exactly the same place. Dolphins use this to send and receive information in their aquatic home.

Like the dolphins, we humans send and receive information constantly. The pineal gland deciphers this information. People whose third eye centers are developed, or sensitive, are capable of picking up information literally "on the air waves" from people and are also capable of interpreting this information consciously. We receive universal, global, and individual waves of energy as an ongoing process, as we react to the world we live in, and it reacts to us.

The electrical activity is unique to each being. We each have our own waves, or "vibrations." Furthermore, these vibrations are created and emitted from the individual aura itself. The aura is the electromagnetic force field that surrounds and pervades every living being. It can be described as a substance resembling pure energy, thought, or light. Perhaps it is a combination of all three.

In the early 1960s two Russian scientists, Semyon and Valentin Kirlian, discovered that they could photograph the aura with special techniques. They discovered not only that the aura itself exists, but that changes occur firstly on the aura before they manifest onto the solid body of the object (Tompkins and Bird, 1989).

Plants, animals, and humans have fine sheaths of sub-atomic or protoplasmic energy that interpenetrates the solid physical bodies of molecules and atoms. In most of the major world religions as well the religions that pre-date recorded history, this sheath was expressed as belief in a "soul" or "ethereal" body. In ancient Egypt, ka was the name given to the spirit double. The ka was known as a mirror of the physical body, but composed of finer matter. The Azande tribe in Africa believes that everyone has an ethereal double, which they call the mbisimo. In Burma, the double is called the Butterfly. The Bacairis of South America simply talk of a "shadow" that leaves the body during sleep and finally at death.

It is through the ethereal double—the aura—that we are able to send and receive information to and from our environment and beyond. In this way, clairvoyants, mediums, psychics, and tarot readers intercept and inter-pret these waves or vibrations.

The left brain deals with logic and form. It is the right brain that connects us to our superconscious. Indeed, the key to divining lies in the ability to still the left brain and conscious daily thoughts, and enter the right brain by altering brain waves to alpha, using simple relaxation or concentration techniques. Clear your mind, relax, and focus on the object of your inquiry. In this way, you are able pick up information from beyond your five senses.

Attempts at stilling and pacifying the left brain do not always come easily. However, the more practiced you get at altering your brain pattern in order to access the super-conscious, the easier it becomes.

THE TAROT

Of all the systems of divination that exist to this day, surely, without bias, the tarot remains the most enchanting and the most popular of all time.

With its symbolic images touching our imaginations, and its intuitive wisdom ready to unfold for us, the tarot has never lost its magic, despite its many hundred years in the cultural wilderness of medieval piety, witch-hunts, and religious bigotry. Perhaps the very visual nature of the tarot has assured it such popularity. One has no need of language when meditating on its colorful, mysterious, and symbolic images. "Every picture tells a story" is no truer said than of the tarot. What other form of divination is so colorful, vivid, and evocative?

Connecting intuitively to its sacred and eternal images we are taken all the more quickly to the world of imagination and symbols, where dreams are woven and reality recorded. Something deep within the soul itself responds automatically to these simple but profound images. It is as though the soul sees itself in a mirror when we gaze upon these archetypal scenes of birth, life, and death. Of all the things that can befall us during our earth-life journeys, the tarot has them already portrayed for us to call upon when in need of help, advice, or confirmation of some action that may affect us for better or worse.

Consulting the tarot when in need of psychological guidance is no stranger than looking at a map when we are lost, or need to find our way in a strange town. Indeed, the tarot itself is a map of our lives. Our happiness, our joys, our sorrows, our struggles are all written in the tarot, and are there for us to draw upon when we need it.

But, where does the tarot come from, and how does it work?

Many theories exist as to the origins of the tarot. Some think it to be the work of European gypsies, and some accredit it to the ancient Egyptians. The truth is, no one actually knows.

Card games, long associated with divinatory practices, entered Europe from the Arabic East in the thirteenth century, part of a wave of old manuscripts and magical beliefs. The first recorded use of tarot as a game of cards appears in Northern Italy in the Court of Ferrara in 1442. The very same game, Quattrocento, is played in Southern Europe and Northern Africa to this day, using a fifteenth-century deck called the Tarot de Marseilles.

Fifteenth-century Romany gypsies seem to be responsible for the spread of the game throughout Europe. By 1781 Antoine Court de Gebelin, a French clergyman and student of mythology, concluded that the tarot was actually the lost Egyptian Book of Thoth, the key to the hidden mysteries of a vanished civilization. The symbols of the cards, Court de Gebelin maintained, were representative of all life, capable of unlimited combinations.

By the early nineteenth century, the tarot had come to the attention of Eliphas Levi, born in Spain in 1810 in humble circumstances, but destined to rise to become an occultist of high repute. Once a priest and journalist, Levi became a magician and occultist and devoted himself to searching for the "key of keys," a system that would unite all magical practices. Levi found the answer in the tarot and identified the 22 Major Arcana with the 22 letters of the Hebrew alphabet, which in turn were the essence of the ancient mystical system of the Kabbalah.

In his book *Rue de la Haute Magique*, he claimed, "The universal key of magical works is that of all ancient religious dogmas, the key of the Kabbalah, the Bible and the little key of Solomon. Among the ancients, the use of this system was permitted only to the high priests. The absolute hieroglyphic science has for its basis an alphabet of which all the gods are letters, all the letters ideas, and the ideas numbers, and all the numbers perfect signs."

By 1887, three master members of an English Masonic order, A.F.A Woodford, Dr. Woodman, and a Dr. Westcott, and a Scottish mason, MacGregor Mathers, formed the Order of the Golden Dawn. The Golden Dawn attempted to synthesize Levi's work into their own, linking the letters of the Hebrew alphabet to the planets and zodiacal signs.

Although the members of the Golden Dawn were impressed by Levi's work, they chose to alter his original allocations by removing the Fool from the bottom of the deck and placing it at the top, thereby moving all the cards down one.

Aleister Crowley joined the Golden dawn in 1898. By the time he left to establish his own order, the Argenteum

Astrum in 1905, he was ready to design his own deck. He himself made further dubious changes to the allocations of the tarot to the Kabbalistic Tree of Life. His system has been used in nearly every deck until this day.

No one, however, seems any wiser as to the actual origins of the tarot. For my part, I intuitively believe that the tarot originated in Atlantis, where it was a means of preserving vital and intricate astrological information that would have been lost when tidal waters of the last Ice Age finally buried this primal civilization under the sea.

Atlantis, that mythical land first described by Plato, was perhaps the original "Garden of Eden," a race of super-people living in a Golden Age. The ruins of Atlantis have yet to be found, and its existence yet to be substantiated. However, a giant flood that covered much of the earth's surface was recorded (for example, in the Bible) in every part of the world simultaneously. Perhaps the same flood destroyed an entire continent and an entire civilization. Thus, when the surviving Atlanteans arrived in ancient Egypt they brought the tarot with them.

Of course, I have absolutely no proof whatsoever to substantiate this theory, and a theory it must remain. Suffice it to say, that whatever the origins of the tarot may be, and however far back in time the tarot was conceived, it is surely mystical by nature. It is of true credit to whomsoever originated the cards that the tarot survives intact to this day.

SYMBOLISM AND
THE UNCONSCIOUS

What is a symbol and how does it affect the unconscious mind?

Simply put, symbolism is a visual language with the power to transcend the conscious mind (left brain) and stimulate or activate the unconscious (right brain).

Although language as we now know it represents things, places, and people with letters; before written and spoken language evolved, simple sounds and symbols had to suffice for communication purposes.

For example, to express the concept of "money," I could draw a gold coin, which we would commonly recognize as a symbol for money. It might also imply wealth, luxury, power, and authority.

Symbols, being visual by nature, also express deeper concepts for which no one word suffices.

The most obvious form of symbolism occurs in visual art. A painting is able to describe many things by form and color alone. Indeed, much of the information we receive about our world is visual, and it is only natural that visual images have the power to both convey and evoke deep and complex ideas and emotions.

Symbolism also represents organic, cellular, and atomic forms. The conscious mind has no reference for these forms, and yet they appear spontaneously in various works of art—especially those of a spiritual nature.

The ancient Buddhist art of painting sacred mandalas and yantras uses symbols to invoke spiritual energies within the viewer by symbolic and deeply effective images. Mandalas and yantras from India and Tibet use symbolic geometrical shapes to convey the concept that everything exists between various fields of energy. The shapes most frequently used are circles, squares, and triangles.

Among the most profound of these symbolic images is the Tantric Buddhist Shri Yantra. This is one of the most sacred yantras in Buddhism and is said to represent the moment of creation, and is linked to the sacred sound "om."

While working with a tonoscope, a machine that transforms sounds into a visual image on a video screen, Dr. Hans Jenny discovered that when the sacred Hindu word Om was recited, the pattern emerged of a perfect circle filled with concentric triangles and squares. The pattern coincided with the frequency pattern of diminishing harmonics, and the pattern was also identical to that of the Shri Yantra. Dr. Jenny's work was inspired by the eighteenth-century German physicist Ernest Chiadni, who first scattered sand on steel discs and observed the changing patterns produced when various notes were played on a violin (Rose, 1987).

The relationship between sound and the creation of matter is referred to in both Hindu and Christian literature. Om is said to have been the word (sound, or vibration) that God uttered to bring forth the materialized universe. In the New Testament, we are told, "In the Beginning was the Word, and the Word was with God and the word was God" (John 1:1).

In the microcosmic world, all matter is in a state of vibration and, according to physicist Dr. Donald Hatch, "We are finding that the universe is composed not of matter, but of music." No wonder that music has the power to transform us, to touch our very souls, taking us to different levels of consciousness. The Baroque composers believed that the universe has a sacred geometry and that these "Golden Means," the exact ratios and proportions of creation, could be reproduced in art and music.

Certain images also take on symbolic significance as perceived by the individual and related to personal memories (conscious or unconscious). These memories may be either individual or collective.

Psychologist Carl Gustav Jung described symbols as falling in three main categories: personal, cultural, and universal. For instance, a personal symbol for you might be the teddy bear that you won at a fair, reminding you of happy times. A cultural symbol may be a dragon, which is considered auspicious in the East, but negative in the West. A universal symbol transcends both and is stored in what Jung termed the "collective unconscious" in each individual being.

We may have no conscious realization of the meaning of symbolic forms. Certainly no tonoscope existed at the time when sacred art was created thousands of years ago.

How then, did the images manifest themselves? However far apart our early cultures were, each of them adopted similar symbolic forms of communication, at the start of the Paleolithic Age, when cave paintings began to appear some 30,000 years ago. Psychologists report that similar images also spontaneously appeared in artistic works of patients with no knowledge of Eastern art or philosophy.

According to Jung's theory on the collective unconscious, all human beings possess a collective memory that has been passed on through the generations. These memories are the net result of our collective genetic humanity and exist within our own subconscious. They speak a language of their own.

Shapes and colors are fundamental in symbolism and certain (if not all) geometric shapes can have a definite affect on the observer. This knowledge is often incorporated into the building of churches, temples, and other places of worship.

By the time Stonehenge was erected over 6,000 years ago, the circle had become the most commonly used mystical symbol. The circle is a reflection of the entire universe. Its periphery represents time-bound existence, and the center represents an infinite and sacred point. The circle remains an accepted symbol all over the world representing divinity, creation, unity, and infinity. The spiral, too, is a universal symbol representing energy flowing in a spiral form.

The art of Feng Shui is an ancient Chinese system of

arranging objects in harmonious order, with the understanding that the energy generated by the interrelation-
ships of physical objects has a powerful affect on anyone
within that space. The Chinese love of Feng Shui was so
great that they even sculpted relevant shapes into the
landscape to encourage a flow of positive energy.

The great pyramids of Egypt were also built on precise
sacred geometric and mathematical formulae, and no
man-made instrument can measure the unusual energies
that exist within them.

We all have universal reactions to color, all of which
have different wavelengths. Blue, for instance, is known
to be calming; red is stimulating, and so on. The colors of
the One World deck are naturally associated with different planets and signs to add even greater symbolic and
healing power to the cards themselves. The correct use of
color is vital to bring dynamism and healing energy to
the deck and to stimulate the viewer in a positive and
nourishing way.

ASTROLOGY AND REINCARNATION

At the point immediately prior to the "Big Bang," which is the beginning of the universe as we know it, all matter was contained in a singularity, that is, a point where all the laws of physics as we know them break down. At the precise moment that the Big Bang occurred, immense amounts of matter began expanding into space and slowly, over billions of years, this cosmic matter began to condense into stars, planets, and all life-forms as we know them, including ourselves. (In Hindu literature the Big Bang is known as "The Divine Breath," and ancient Sanskrit texts describe the universe as expanding and contracting at regular intervals.)

Once the universe had condensed sufficiently, it produced our solar system, with its nine known planets: Mercury, Venus, Earth with its Moon, Mars, Jupiter, Saturn, Neptune, Uranus, and Pluto. All of these share a common orbit around a giant star called simply—the Sun.

One of the most fundamental characteristics of a planetary body is its state of magnetization. The Earth, as well as all the other planets in our solar system, has a network of electrical currents flowing in its deep interior. In other words, the Earth and the other planets are huge electromagnets. As the planets orbit the sun, their force fields interact and directly affect the Earth's magnetosphere, which in turn affects the magnetic fields (auras, or ethereal bodies) of every single life form on Earth—humans, animals, and plants.

To visualize what happens when planetary magnetic fields inter-react, imagine a calm pond. Throw a stone in the pond and watch the ripples as they travel outwards from the point of impact. Next, throw two stones in at equidistant points and watch how the two sets of "waves" interact with each other. Lastly, throw ten pebbles in at various points and see how the "waves" create various patterns when they overlap each other.

This is how the lines of magnetism might look as they are emitted from the planets that dance through space, orbiting the heavens.

Each planet has its own unique magnetic force field, which has a particular effect on life on Earth. Each force field, in combination with the others, produces the infinite variations in electromagnetic activity necessary to create and sustain life on Earth as we know it.

As well as emitting various electromagnetic forces, the planets also emit sound waves, and each planet is esoterically assigned a different note of the musical scale. When the U.S. space probe Voyager 2 approached Saturn, it picked up noise from the magnetosphere of Saturn, which was beamed back to Earth. When these noises were sped up and played through a musical synthesizer, the waves were found to consist of a distinct melody (Starck, 1997).

As we saw in the experiments with the tonoscope, sound has the ability to organize matter into distinct patterns. Perhaps the resonance, harmonies, and vibrations that the planets constantly emit had a creative effect on the primordial oceans of the Earth, thus enabling organic structures to arise from the rich biochemical soup of the oceans, in accordance with the various musical symphonies the planets were creating.

The concept of a sacred or divine sound that gave rise to the materialization of the universe is described in both Hindu and biblical literature. Pythagoras and Plato observed that the ratios between the notes on the musical scale are identical to the ratio of the mean orbital distances of one planet to another. These orbits become progressively greater by the ratio of two to one as they increase in distance from the Sun. Earth, therefore, is twice as far away from Mercury as Venus and Mars is twice as far away from the Earth. This numerical relationship continues to the outer reaches of the solar system and Pluto.

In the same way that the musical scale, composed as it is of a limited number of notes, can produce an infinite variety of musical compositions, the planetary "tones" are also able to define and "orchestrate" life systems on Earth, affecting the organization of matter into distinct patterns and shapes. Each planet has a different job to perform, as each note has a different job to perform in a chord, a song, or a symphony.

Each of the planets also has a direct influence on the chakras and the glandular systems of organic life-forms, and each sign and planet is said to rule a different part of the physical, mental, emotional, and spiritual functions.

The magnetic pull and vibrational tone of the Moon, for instance, has a gravitational effect on fluids producing, for example, the tides of the oceans. Scientists have recently measured the gravitational pull of the Moon in a cup of tea. Imagine how much more the pull on our bodies, which are nearly seventy percent water. Does this explain the tendency to "lunacy" at full Moons, when the magnetic pull of the Moon is strongest—and the crime rate highest?

Through its gravitational affect on fluids, the Moon has a direct affect on cycles of glandular activity in the body. In particular, the human female menstrual cycle is 28 days long, the same time it takes the Moon to orbit the Earth. Marine life also synchronizes mating and spawning habits to the lunar cycles. In astrology, the Moon is said to rule the water sign of Cancer, which rules motherhood and birth.

During the early seventies, Dr. Jonas (a Czech physician researching female fertility) discovered that human females could spontaneously release an ovum once a month, regardless of their normal menstrual cycle, at the exact moment that the Sun and Moon formed the same angle at the woman's birth. For instance, if you were born at a new Moon, then on every new Moon this phenomenon would occur. He subsequently developed a system of birth control, based on the normal menstrual cycle and the lunar cycle, which is 97 percent effective.

He further discovered that the Moon's position in a woman's birth chart determined, also with 97 percent accuracy, the sex of her children. As the Moon transited positive (fire and air) and negative (water and earth) sectors of the zodiac, it would favor either the X or Y chromosome magnetically, in alternating periods of approximately 2.5 days.

The Moon is slowly drifting away from Earth's orbit, and sometime in the very distant future—millions of years from now—the Moon will break away from the Earth's gravitational field altogether. The tides of the oceans will swell, covering the Earth in gigantic waves and floods. When they eventually settle down, there will be no tides, oceanic or otherwise. So far as we know, without the tides, the oceans of the world will become stagnant pools, incapable of sustaining life.

We depend on the cycles and magnetism of the Moon just as we depend on the Sun. The Sun's rays, both visible and invisible, maintain life on Earth. Without the Sun, we simply would not exist at all.

The Sun emits heat and light and other forms of electromagnetic radiation. This outpouring of ionized gases and the associated magnetic field is called the solar wind. The solar wind is hot plasma, an electrically neutral mixture of ions whose source is the Sun's corona. This gas flows outward at a speed of approximately 450 kilometers per second to distances twice the orbit of Pluto. Because of the

Sun's rotation, the emissions form an Archimedean spiral.

When the solar wind hits the Earth's magnetosphere, it distorts it with enormous force, depending on the speed and density of solar emissions. The varying amount of solar emissions (magnetic plasma) that enter Earth's atmosphere will therefore have a direct effect on the magnetic fields of all other life forms, including us.

Recent research conducted at NASA in the United States has proved that when solar radiation is at its strongest, heart attacks (among other events) became more frequent. In astrology, the Sun rules the sign of Leo, which rules the heart.

Each planet has its own energy or vibration and unique chemical composition, which can influence life on Earth. The planets also affect each other as they orbit the Sun, creating varying angular relationships to us.

In 1951, J.H. Nelson, an engineer with RCA, was asked to investigate a problem RCA was having with its radio reception quality, which seemed to vary with Sun spot activity. After careful research, Nelson discovered that the days when interference was at its worst were days when any one of the planets formed an angle of 0, 90, or 180 degrees to the Sun. Since planetary movement is entirely predictable, this knowledge enabled RCA to forecast days on which reception would be affected—in advance.

In exactly the same way as Nelson was able to determine times of future activity by calculating the paths of the planets, astrologers are able to chart future events. By drawing a map of the heavens at the time of birth, astrologers are able to describe an individual and his or her life's journey in detail, interpreting the relationship between the positions of the planets at birth and their continuing orbital relationships to each other in relation to the original birth chart.

The relationships of the planets to each other and us are crucial to the understanding of the power of astrology as a divinatory science. However, this is the very point at which many will nervously question the concept of destiny versus free will.

Albert Einstein once said, "I cannot believe God plays dice with the Universe." Many do believe however, that our lives are simply a series of random events, whilst others believe in fate or destiny. So, do we have free will or are we bound by fate? To explain this let me give you a simple analogy.

I am waiting at a bus station—I need to make a journey. I must choose between buses A, B, or C. Each bus will take its own specific route, and I am entirely free to choose which journey I wish to make. However, once I have made my decision and boarded the bus, I have no choice but to follow the route I have already chosen. (Unless I get off.)

To continue our analogy, when I am at the bus station, I am in my pre-birth consciousness and I must decide what particular life journey I need to make to continue my karmic lessons. Once I have determined which journey

I need to make, however, I must incarnate back onto the material plane (earth) and follow that route implicitly.

This illustrates both free will and preordained destiny—and the way they operate in our lives is through the phenomena of reincarnation.

The theory of reincarnation states that all of our previous actions will result in reactions that we ourselves have already set in motion in previous lives. Until we reach perfection, we must repeatedly reincarnate on Earth to learn our karmic lessons. Our karma, which we set in motion in previous time, is still unfolding.

In his third Law of Motion, physicist Sir Isaac Newton stated categorically, that "every action has an equal and opposite reaction." This universal law is known as the law of cause and effect, and is referred to in Buddhist literature as the law of karma. In the New Testament Christ also makes a simple reference to this universal law when he tells us, "As you sow, so shall ye reap."

The theory of reincarnation and karma is not restricted to Eastern religions and philosophies like Hinduism and Buddhism. It appears consistently in most, if not all, of the world religions. In Africa the Yoruba believed that reincarnation took place solely within the family. If they recognized a transcendent soul, or ori, it would be given a special name. Babatunde meant that "father has returned" and for girls, Iyatunde "mother has returned" (Mitchell, 1977).

The concept of reincarnating back into the immediate family is not unknown in the theory of reincarnation, but individuals may also choose to reincarnate in soul groups, as well as continuing intense personal relationships with old "soul mates." These continuing relationships may be for a specific purpose, either individual or collective, and are a direct result of individual and group karma.

The theory of reincarnation is present in the majority of the world's religions since the dawn of philosphy, and is so intrinsic in human culture that it pre-dates recorded history. The many recorded testaments of millions of ordinary people who have had past life memories add to a body of evidence in favor of reincarnation, too great to ignore. The detailed accounts of events and other histori-cal data could not have been obtained under any other circumstances.

In her book *Yesterday's Children*, Jenny Cockell describes vivid childhood memories of a past life, in which she was "Mary," a poor Irish woman who died at the age of 33, leaving six young children behind her. "Mary's" death trauma of leaving her children was so great that she vowed to return, and she was incarnated as Jenny Cockell ten years later. In her childhood, Jenny was obsessed with memories of her past life, and she drew maps and diagrams of where "Mary" lived. Jenny also gave the name of her then husband and the story of his life in the army. By her teens, Jenny had found records of her life as "Mary" and the town in which she lived. All matched her childhood memories. She was re-united with her six children.

It is not uncommon for children to consciously remember details of past lives, and there are thousands of such cases. But adults, more often than not, experience past life memory through dreams, regression, or hypnosis. Liz Howard, a scientist at ICI in Cheshire, England, is a typical case in point.

For Liz, a vivid and haunting dream about an old Tudor manor house was the start of an unexpected series of events that eventually took her back, under hypnosis, to a former life as Elizabeth Fitton. Born at Gawsworth Hall in 1503, and later a handmaiden to Anne Boleyn, wife of King Henry VIII, Liz was able to describe in detail original features of the local parish church, and features of Gawsworth Hall that were known only to the current owners. All her personal details as Elizabeth Fitton were later confirmed by records at Gawsworth Hall itself. Although Liz Howard still remains skeptical about her experiences, one thing still intrigues her: Elizabeth Fitton was her own maiden name in this life.

Commenting on her experiences with hypnosis, Liz said that although she never lost sight of who and where she was when she was actually under hypnosis, she seemed to be able to view—with detachment—her emotional past life experiences.

The number of people who are reporting verifiable past life experiences is growing daily. Past life experience or recall is not limited to any one faith or religion, or any one group or nationality of people. These experiences are being recorded all over the world, to people of every race and religion, and cultural, social and economic group.

The concept of a foreordained destiny occurs in many religions. In Ghana it is believed that destiny is determined by the way in which the new being takes leave of the creator before birth. The concepts of "judgment," "soul," and "afterlife" are other recurring themes in world religions.

The individual astrological birth chart can be said to describe the current individual life journey (or destiny of the incoming soul) and represents the precise point at which the incarnating one has chosen to reenter the world to continue its karmic journey.

When we understand the law of karma, and we understand that our own actions will eventually return to us, we become masters of our future destinies. We now understand the law of cause and effect and become fully conscious and responsible for our own actions, realizing how the effects of those actions will ripple out into time/space and return to us one day, eventually. If I walk east from any point on the planet, I will return to my original starting point from the west. In the same way, the cyclic nature of the universe sends back to us the very thoughts, acts, and vibrations we create.

Astrology, then, is the study of cycles—both universal and individual. The planets are cosmic cyclic regulators, all of which affect and describe life on Earth. At some point in the distant past, all the knowledge of the heavenly movements and archetypal possibilities, as defined by astrology, were recorded on paper in visual form and this ultimately holy book is known as the tarot.

THE KABBALAH AND NUMEROLOGY

A unified field theory, that is, a single theorem that would explain all the laws of the universe in one complete system, has long eluded modern science. Scientific research into the subatomic world, however, has revealed that atoms, subatomic particles, and dynamic patterns do not exist as isolated occurrences, but as an integral part of an inseparable whole.

The Kabbalah could be described as the unified field theory of an ancient metaphysical tradition which, it is said, was first given to the archangels, who gave it to the angels, who in turn gave it to Moses on Mount Sinai after he received the Ten Commandments from God. The first four books of the Kabbalah form the first four chapters of the Old Testament. The Kabbalah is inherent in both Judaism and Christianity.

The Kabbalah, which literally translated means "to receive" or "to reveal," has both a written and an oral tradition. There are three main written texts. The *Sepher Yetzirah* describes God as indescribable. The *Zohar*, commonly referred to as the Book of Splendor, defines the universe as an interconnected mass of particles governed by a higher force. The *Sepher Bahir*, known as the Book of Brilliance, describes the universe as a multilayered reality in which all parts are connected and governed by a higher law.

The teachings of the Kabbalah are encompassed in

the Kabbalistic Tree of Life, a schematic diagram that represents the underlying blueprint and principles of creation. The Tree of Life describes how God (energy, spirit) manifests the physical universe (matter) in a series of mystical and alchemical processes through ten Sephiroth or spheres.

Simply speaking, spirit (En Soph), which can in its essence be viewed as pure energy, consciousness, or light, is slowed down through a series of transformers, to its slowest vibration, which is perceived as matter (Malkuth).

The Kabbalah is not only an objective theory that relates to universal creation, but can be seen to be a subjective reality. It is a divine geometric and mathematical blueprint for all creation, the totality of which exists within all manifestations, a microcosm of the whole universe.

In the New Testament, Christ tells his followers that this light (En Soph) exists within us all when he tells us, "Let thine sight be single [a reference to the third eye] and thine whole body shall be full of light" (Luke 11:34). This light can be seen to be the self-same light of En Soph, which exists within all manifested phenomena simultaneously and which is the very essence of creation itself and the formative principle behind every life-form in the entire universe. Being the eldest son of a Jewish family, Jesus would have been fully initiated into the secrets of the Kabbalah.

"Going towards the light" has become a literal experience for millions of people all over the world who have had a so-called near-death experience. This phenomenon has become a daily occurrence now that medical science has enabled people who have just "died" to come back to life. Never in human history has this phenomena become so widespread and so well documented. In nearly every instance of the near death experience, the subject finds him or herself floating above the body and then passing through a long tunnel toward "the light" (En Soph), which is described as a most beautiful divine experience with the most overwhelming feeling of love and peace that the subject has ever experienced. This light can be none other than En Soph itself, which exists in a state of omnipresence within all things. Having come from the light, we must return to it.

The eternal light of En Soph—God, energy, consciousness, spirit—is the causative factor of all manifested phenomena and is behind all creation, universal, human, and atomic. It exists simultaneously within all created phenomena.

In the beginning is En Soph, the endless and boundless one-eternity, infinity and the void. En Soph exists before creation and exists after creation. En Soph causes within itself a vibration that emanates waves of light and sound. Light manifests a visible universe. To create the material universe, a series of transformers are needed to slow down light, but when it reaches a slow enough vibration, it bursts through from the ether in the form of a Big Bang. When the universe has expanded to its fullest potential, it will again come in on itself and return to the invisible dimensions of creation.

In between En Soph and Malkuth are ten Sephiroth, or spheres. These are the transformers needed to slow down En Soph to manifest the material world.

The Holy Kabbalah then, is a schematic diagram of the numerological and mathematical framework needed to create a materialized universe. Every individual form is created on the same universal principles, and these same laws interpenetrate both the macrocosmic and the microcosmic worlds.

The Kabbalah is subdivided into three Pillars—Judgment, Mildness, and Mercy, representing the trinity of spirit, mind, and body. It is subdivided again into Four Worlds, which represent the four elements of fire, water, earth, and air. Seven horizontal levels relate to the seven chakras.

Each Sephirah of the Kabbalah represents a numerological principle of creation, from one to ten, and is equated with one of the ten major planetary influences that shape life on Earth. Through the planetary energies the ten main qualities of the Kabbalah manifest themselves.

The three Pillars can be seen within the three main sections of the tarot, Major Arcana, Minor Arcana, and Court cards. The four worlds are represented as the four elements, or suits, and the ten Sephiroth are represented in the Minor Arcana suits as cards numbered one to ten.

To the occult numerologist, numbers represent the

primal organizing principle that gives structure to the materialized universe. The seasons, the movements of the planets, even harmony in music—are all determined by numerical law. The obvious and undeniable rhythm to life, plain for us all to see, can be measured as cycles, waves, or vibrations. All of which are measured in turn by number. As Pythagoras observed, "All things are number." The laws, rhythms, and cycles of the universe are also definable by number and there are precise mathematical and numerological principles at work beneath the web of creation.

Numbers and numerical law are at the very heart of all creation. Numbers represent the ability of the One (En Soph) to multiply in the same way that an embryo, by a process of cell division and multiplication, becomes a fully formed entity.

The 64 paths on the Tree of Life (32 from En Soph to Malkuth and 32 from Malkuth to En Soph) are synonymous with the 64 hexagrams of the I Ching in ascending order. Therefore the first hexagram of the I Ching, The Creative, is equivalent to The Magician of the tarot.

The meanings of numbers one through ten are as follows:

ONE: THE MONAD
SEPHIRAH: KETHER, THE CROWN

One is the number of creation and unity, the beginning of all things. It also represents authority and leadership, self-reliance, tenacity, and singleness of purpose.

TWO: THE DUAD
SEPHIRAH: CHOKMAH, WISDOM

Two is the number of diversity, duality, and balance. It expresses opposites: night and day, male and female, hot and cold. It also represents sensitivity and intuition, justice and sociability.

THREE: THE TRIAD
SEPHIRAH: BINAH, UNDERSTANDING

Three represents creativity and procreation. Comprehensiveness and fulfillment. It also suggests faith, energy, optimism, confidence, adventurousness, and exuberance.

FOUR: THE TETRAD
SEPHIRAH: CHESED, MERCY

Four represents solidity and stability, firm foundations. It also represents opportunities and practicality, loyalty, honesty, and willpower.

FIVE: THE PENTAD
SEPHIRAH: GEBURAH, STRENGTH

Five is the number of awareness, intelligence, and variety. It also represents expansion, experience, curiosity, freedom, courage, and vivaciousness.

SIX: THE HEXAD
SEPHIRAH: TIPHARETH, BEAUTY

Six represents ideals, truth, justice, and beauty. It also represents perfect harmony and completion, honesty, faithfulness, and responsibility.

SEVEN: THE HEPTAD
SEPHIRAH: NETZACH, VICTORY

Symbol of good fortune and wisdom, the number seven also represents peace, satisfaction, solitude, contemplation, and responsibility.

EIGHT: THE OGDOAD
SEPHIRAH: HOD, SPLENDOR

Number eight is original and inventive. It also represents new thought, psychology, and an inquiring mind, power, control, and mastery.

NINE: THE ENNEAD
SEPHIRAH: YESOD, FOUNDATION

Nine is the number of aspiration, spirituality, and perfection. It is also a number of justice, tolerance, and spiritual love.

TEN: THE DECAD
SEPHIRAH: MALKUTH, THE KINGDOM

Ten is the first composite number in numerology and represents completion.

In *The Tenth Dimension*, prominent Japanese quantum physicist Michio Kaku writes about his theory and belief that the universe is composed not of four, but of ten dimensions. His rough diagram of how these dimensions interconnect is remarkably similar to the Tree of Life.

Many other discoveries within physics and quantum mechanics are surely on their way to verifying the ancient claims of mystics and seers. Science is slowly coming, by its own path, to the inevitable conclusions regarding the creation and nature of the universe. These same conclusions have been written and recorded, sometimes symbolically (sometimes secretly) in the foundations of many great religions of the world.

The Kabbalah and the Tree of Life have been preserved sacredly throughout the ages and remain intact as a system of learning and understanding that connects God, humanity, and the universe in a comprehensive and interdependent reality. We must surely thank the descendants of those who followed Moses out of Sinai so long ago, and who faithfully preserved this ancient metaphysical doctrine, for the ultimate benefit and betterment of humankind.

The Kabbalah may reveal to us the route back to Godhead, but only we can take the first step.

THE NEW AGE

An astrological age is a period of time in which the evolutionary trends on Earth are determined by a particular sign of the zodiac. The effects of that age will be prominent in global culture, development, evolution, art, symbolism, philosophy, and religion.

Each age is caused by the precession of the equinoxes, which in turn is caused by the rotation and tilt of the Earth on its own axis. If you were to draw an imaginary line through the earth exiting at the North Pole, and note the direction in which it was pointing, it would be pointing to one of the twelve signs of the zodiac.

As the Earth's axis wobbles, that line moves throughout the zodiac, taking a full 25,920 years to complete the whole cycle of all twelve signs. The precession of the equinoxes goes backward through the signs. Therefore, the coming New Age of Aquarius will take over from the Age of Pisces. The Earth remains in each sign for approximately 2,160 years.

Each age, ruled by different signs and planets, "sets the tone" for evolutionary trends. If, as we have seen, matter is organized by sound, then the planetary cycles and emissions may be the governing principle of creation and evolution of life on Earth.

Cycles and rhythms are all intrinsic in creation. One cycle that is the subject of much enthusiasm and speculation at the moment is the Age of Aquarius, or the New Age.

The sign of Aquarius is said to govern electricity, technology, invention, the unusual, and the unexpected. Aquarius—an intellectual fixed Air sign—is ruled by the planet Uranus (discovered in 1781), which is a higher octave of Mercury.

The discovery of Uranus heralded the dawn of the industrial revolution, the discovery of electricity, technology, and scientific development—all of which transformed an agricultural world into a technological society, in a relatively short period of time. In one hundred years, we have gone from horse and cart to space travel. These are all indications of the approaching New Aquarian Age.

Jesus Christ was the prophet or messenger for the New Age of Pisces the Fish, and Jesus in Hebrew means "fish." Christ proclaimed himself a "fisher of men," and his disciples were fishermen. The fish itself was a secret symbol, found in caves and other secluded places, symbolizing the new faith, which encompassed the Piscean qualities of non-materialism, faith, mysticism, humility, and compassion.

The Piscean Age would also, however, have contained qualities of its opposite sign of Virgo the Virgin, and the second central character in Christian mythology is the Virgin Mary. Christ symbolized the New Age of Pisces, and the Virgin Mary symbolized the polar opposite, Virgo, which represents reason and analysis—both of which are quite clearly visible in recent history as scientific reasoning and logic.

In Britain, the arrival of the Age of Pisces was symbolized

in the legend of St. George killing the dragon. St. George and his red cross symbolized the new religion, Christianity, and the dragon symbolized the old Pagan religions that were being systematically eradicated. In Pagan Britain, ley lines, or energy lines, were also known as dragon lines.

Christianity has dominated Western religious thought for nearly 2,000 years, spearheaded by the church, which originated in Rome and was spread through Europe by invading Roman armies. The Roman Church dominated in Britain until the reign of King Henry VIII, who broke away from papal authority to divorce his first wife and marry Anne Boleyn.

The Church of England has continued to dominate English religious thought and practice until this day. However, in November 1996, the Church of England issued a report "In Search of Faith." The report stated that in the U.K., only 14 percent of people attend church regularly, but a staggering 75 percent of the population admitted to believing in God and, surprisingly, reincarnation.

The Church blamed astrology, New Age, and Neo-Pagan religions, as well as indigenous folk religions for its decline, and it warned against a return to "darkness and superstition" and a "pick and mix" philosophy. The decline of the Church indeed coincides with the ending of the Piscean Age.

But when does the New Age actually begin?

According to the Mayans, who had the most precise

cosmological calendar, the current Age of Pisces is due to end in 2008. However, according to the Hebrew calendar, the current age ends in 2012. Other equally qualified sources put the New Age beginning around the year 2160, and some go as late as 2343. Some astrologers think it has already begun.

Unfortunately, it looks as though we just don't know exactly when Pisces ends and Aquarius begins. I personally believe that (at the time of writing this book) we are still on the Pisces side of the cusp. I further believe that we will have clear signs, when the time comes, that we have moved into a New Age.

The signs that we are fast approaching the Age of Aquarius are already here: space travel, science, technology, genetic engineering, UFO phenomena, near death experiences, astrology, computers, New Age religions, telepathy, ESP, satellite television, and mobile phones—all herald the dawn of the New Aquarian Age.

The Aquarian Age may take us far into the reaches of space and technology, virtual reality and genetic engineering, but I believe that Leo, the opposite sign to Aquarius, will balance out the detached inventiveness of the New Age and provide the Aquarian age with some "heart." Otherwise we might end up on a barren planet run by robots and computers.

The sign of Leo, which governs creativity, entertainment, love, and pleasure, will make sure that we can all let our hair down and enjoy ourselves in a natural and loving way. (We first saw evidence of this in the 1960s.) I believe we will see an end to puritanism, a Virgoan quality, and the sexual and cultural taboos that have dominated Western society for so long.

Perhaps we will even see a return to Sun and nature worship in one form or another, with a much greater appreciation of life in general. The leisure and entertainment fields such as art, dance, film, and music will flourish in the New Age.

Perhaps we will also have the time to redevelop some of the communal traditions and rituals of society that have been so important in maintaining a healthy culture for so long in our collective history, and that our tribal ancestors had down to a fine art. Many of these rituals are based on communal worship and celebration, which are absolutely vital to our psychic wholeness and health.

Music has always played a vital role in religious and ritualized celebrations, and as we have already seen, music may even have the direct ability to influence matter. It is now known that musical sounds and vibrations are important in supplying and maintaining vital life energies within individual beings.

In ancient tribal cultures, music was an integral part of communal life, and music and dancing were seen as vital to the health of the individual and the community. It is no wonder that today's raves and festivals have become so essential in replacing lost communal musical rituals, and that our musical celebrities, our "stars," are elevated to semi-religious status.

It is a sad indictment of Western society that we have become so divorced from our roots and the meaning of those roots, that such essential religious recreational activities are frowned upon, repressed, and crushed so ignorantly by the authorities. Another common feature of ancient religious and spiritual rituals was the use of psychoactive plants as a means of inducing altered states of consciousness, to facilitate religious, mystical, or transcendental experiences, and even to contact the spirit worlds or ancestors for revelations and visions. The instinctive revival of the use of psychoactive substances as a means of inducing altered states of consciousness is highly evident in Western society today. These plant potions appear to have the ability to stimulate the right side of the brain.

Although these practices were encouraged in many spiritual rituals in older tribal societies, they are distinctly frowned on in the West, where such practices are considered criminal offenses. However, in June 1998 the Church of England issued a new report, written by the Reverend Kenneth Leech, that calls for a debate on the decriminalization of drugs in the U.K. saying that "drug taking is closely linked to the quest for a richer inner spiritual life and the profound emptiness at the heart of our society."

A common feature of drug-induced mystical experience is a feeling of well-being and transcendence, or oneness with the universe. The transcendental experience is a state of consciousness acknowledged in Buddhism and other philosophical and meditational teachings.

Research conducted by Dr. Michael Persinger at the University of Laurentean in Canada revealed that stimulation of the temporal lobe in the human brain with electromagnetic forces brought about a "mystical experience," regardless of the religious beliefs of the subject. Dr. Persinger claims that he can induce a religious experience by electrical stimulation of the brain in any and everyone. People exposed to lightning also report mystical sensations.

Dr. Persinger's research indicates that deep within the brain there is a mechanism for connecting us with inner religious or mystical forces or experiences. We merely require some sort of a trigger, whether electromagnetic or organic. Dr. Persinger has proven that the potential for mystical experience exists within all of us. This is surely echoed in Christ's famous words, "The kingdom of heaven lies within. Seek and ye shall find; knock and the door shall open" (Matthew 7:7).

Modern science is now coming to inadvertently prove these ancient religious beliefs and claims. To acknowledge the truths behind the supernatural and mystical contained in many of the world's ancient religions and philosophies is perhaps the biggest challenge of the coming New Age and one which, if accomplished, has the power to unite all people in a common understanding.

Throughout generations we have individually and

collectively exchanged our true inner spirituality, our traditions, and our rituals for scientific and technological materialism. We are now suffering the consequences.

In *Alien Dawn* Colin Wilson documents the evidence of extraterrestrial contact with Earth, and their relationship to human evolution. He writes, "Man has undoubtedly reached a crisis point in his evolution. In the past 3,000 years or so he has developed a down-to-earth, practical consciousness, which has made him the most dominant species on our planet. Unfortunately, however, it has also brought him to a kind of cul-de-sac in his evolution. Trapped in this narrow material consciousness, he has reached a point where he might destroy himself through pollution, overpopulation, and misuse of his scientific achievements. He has never been so urgently in need of some kind of guidance" (Wilson, 1998).

Many share the view that humankind is on the verge of some great evolutionary leap in consciousness—one desperately needed if we are to evolve and survive as a species. With our planet now so close to ecological disaster, only by reuniting with God, humanity, and nature can we hope to survive. If we continue to treat Mother Earth and all her children, be they human, animal, or otherwise, with disrespect, we have only ourselves to blame if we destroy her, and she us.

As we get ever closer to the New Age, all our systems of spirituality, philosophy, and religion will experience change, renewal, and revival. But positive change is to be embraced, not feared, and should be welcomed as a refreshing complement to that which already exists both culturally and historically.

Let us hope that the Age of Aquarius brings us all closer to ourselves, closer to each other, and closer to our creator God, and that we will truly live together with sympathy and understanding.

Let the New Age commence.

PART TWO

THE ONE WORLD TAROT

The One World Tarot deck is a fusion of traditional tarot and modern design. It incorporates astrological, numerological, esoteric, and color symbolism. The cards themselves are essentially symbolic pictorial representations of universal and astrological energies.

The deck expresses as many different aspects of these energies as possible, through the symbolic use of form and color. Each card is linked with its correct astrological counterpart. The following pages describe the traditional meanings of the cards and the astrological interpretations so that you can see the direct relationship of planets, signs, elements, and zodiac subdivisions to each card.

Astrology, intrinsic to the One World deck, describes life on Earth—both great and small. By using a pictorial system in an intuitive way, we can determine influences and trends without the complicated mathematical nuances of astrology.

Those of you who have some astrological knowledge will be able to see for yourselves how the tarot and astrology come together. Those of you with little astrological knowledge may find the One World deck an enjoyable way of learning more about the subject.

Each card of the One World deck describes a different archetypal life situation to which, as humans living on the planet Earth, we are all subject.

The Major Arcana—Planets and Signs

The 22 Major Arcana are linked with the 22 letters of the Hebrew alphabet and the Kabbalistic Tree of Life. There is an alignment with the ten planets and the 12 Zodiac signs.

Aleph	1	Mercury	The Magician
Beth	2	Virgo	The High Priestess
Gimel	3	Libra	The Empress
Daleth	4	Scorpio	The Emperor
He	5	Jupiter	The High Priest
Vau	6	Venus	The Lovers
Zain	7	Sagittarius	The Chariot
Cheth	8	Capricorn	Justice
Teth	9	Aquarius	The Hermit
Jod	10	Uranus	The Wheel of Fortune
Caph	11	Neptune	Strength
Lamed	12	Pisces	The Hanged Man
Mem	13	Aries	The Rebirth
Nun	14	Taurus	Temperance
Samek	15	Saturn	Deliverance
Ayin	16	Mars	The Tower
Fe	17	Gemini	The Star
Tzaddi	18	Cancer	The Moon
Quoph	19	Leo	The Sun
Resh	20	The Moon	Judgment
Shin	21	The Sun	The World
Tau	0	The Earth	The Fool

The Minor Arcana—The Four Elements

The four suits, represented by the four elements, are divided by the decantes (subdivisions) of each sign, and by their numerological powers 1 through 9.

	FIRE Batons	EARTH Coins	AIR Swords	WATER Cups
1	The Element	The Element	The Element	The Element
2	1st Dec Aries	1st Dec Taurus	1st Dec Gemini	1st Dec Cancer
3	2nd Dec Aries	2nd Dec Taurus	2nd Dec Gemini	2nd Dec Cancer
4	3rd Dec Aries	3rd Dec Taurus	3rd Dec Gemini	3rd Dec Cancer
5	1st Dec Leo	1st Dec Virgo	1st Dec Libra	1st Dec Scorpio
6	2nd Dec Leo	2nd Dec Virgo	2nd Dec Libra	2nd Dec Scorpio
7	3rd Dec Leo	3rd Dec Virgo	3rd Dec Libra	3rd Dec Scorpio
8	1st Dec Sagittarius	1st Dec Capricorn	1st Dec Aquarius	1st Dec Pisces
9	2nd Dec Sagittarius	2nd Dec Capricorn	2nd Dec Aquarius	2nd Dec Pisces
10	3rd Dec Sagittarius	3rd Dec Capricorn	3rd Dec Aquarius	3rd Dec Pisces

The Court Cards

The court cards represent the elemental archetypes.

Batons (Fire) .... Aries, Leo, Sagittarius

Coins (Earth) .... Taurus, Virgo, Capricorn

Swords (Air) .... Gemini, Libra, Aquarius

Cups (Water) .... Cancer, Scorpio, Pisces

Kings and Queens .... Mature adults (male and female)

Princes and Princesses .... Youths (male and female)

THE MAJOR ARCANA

1 *The Magician/Mercury* ☿

The ultimate Magician is the creative force that brings all things into conscious manifestation. The Magician continually balances the opposing forces of yin and yang, and the miracle of creation is brought about by this interaction of opposite but complementary forces.

The two halves of the yin-yang symbol can also be said to represent the two halves of the brain, the left and right, active (red) and passive (green). With the brain we send and receive information to and from our environment. The purple background represents the unconscious, the complementary opposite of the conscious.

ASTROLOGICAL INTERPRETATION

Mercury, the closest and swiftest orbiting planet around the Sun, is known in Greek mythology as Hermes, the winged messenger. It is his job to carry and assess information and to communicate ideas.

Mercury has a direct physiological relationship with the brain and nervous system, the lungs, shoulders, arms, hands, and the five senses, which communicate information from the outside world.

Through his relationship and rulership over the sign of Gemini, The Magician governs language, telephones, mail, and all those in the communications fields.

Through his relationship and rulership of the Earth sign of Virgo, Mercury is also nervous, analytical, critical, precise, and a perfectionist. He rules artists, craftspeople, teachers, nurses, and those in associated professions.

Mercury can be said to rule the function of communication and has talent for both the written and spoken word—as in journalists, writers, singers, and speakers—and also deals with short distance journeys, neighbors, brothers, and sisters. Mercury is agile, quick, inquisitive, and detailed.

The negative aspects of Mercury can be unreliability, nervousness, criticalness, emotional coldness, and an inability to mentally relax. They tend to suffer with bronchial or digestive complaints.

TRADITIONAL INTERPRETATION

The Magician has the power to bring things into manifestation. This card symbolizes originality, imagination, self-reliance, resolution, skill, flexibility, dexterity, and craft.

COMMENTARY

The Tarot, Alfred Douglas: "Traditionally the Magician is the Adept who has brought all facets of his being into conscious equilibrium, from the physical to the divine."

The equilibrium to which Alfred Douglas refers is reflected in the perfect equilibrium of the yin-yang symbol—spirit and matter.

Indeed, Mercury rules Gemini, the Twins, which expresses duality and changeability, veering from one "twin" (half) to the other. The yin-yang symbol, like the Twins, is forever in motion, experiencing extremes of feeling, emotion, and thought. The planet Mercury itself shows us only one face, while the other is never seen. One half is perpetually in the light, and one half is perpetually in the dark.

Jung and the Tarot, Sallie Nichols: "The almost hypnotic sweep of [the Magician's hat; referring to the Tarot of Marseilles image] connotes the movement of the opposites, each endlessly changing into the other, as in the Chinese symbol Tai Chi, which shows the ceaseless interaction of yang and yin, the positive and negative forces inherent in all nature. If you concentrate on the

Magician's hat brim by candlelight in the dark of the Moon, he will make it move for you. Seen thus, it becomes the perpetual motion of creation."

The unconscious archetype of The Magician as messenger and sometimes trickster is reflected in the imagery of this card. His influence in our lives lies in the realm of the logical thought processes associated with left-brain activity.

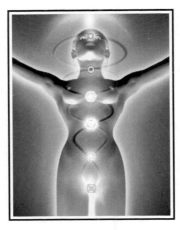

2 The High Priestess/Virgo ♍

The caduceus is a symbol of healing and knowledge associated with Mercury, the planet that rules Virgo. Virgo is the only human figure in the zodiac, and so is the only human figure in the One World Major Arcana.

The intertwining "serpents" symbolize the currents of kundalini energy which flow from heaven (crown chakra) to Earth (base chakra) and back again in opposing currents, known in Vedic literature as ida and pingala, or simply put, positive and negative currents of energy. When these currents are flowing in harmony, or equilibrium, we achieve a state of health. When these universal currents of energy are out of balance, ill health is the result.

ASTROLOGICAL INTERPRETATION

Virgo is the sixth sign of the zodiac and is associated with harvest time. Thus Virgo is often shown as a Virgin with a sheaf of wheat. Wheat must be separated from the chaff, however. Virgo, through its association with detailed analysis, must sort out the intellectual wheat from the chaff. In other words, Virgo is involved in a process of elimination, of purification, and is therefore associated with the digestive tract—the large and small intestine. In the intestines, too, we sort out the useful from the useless, and discard the waste accordingly. With the Virgoan desire for purity and perfection, this sign is associated with all matters connected with health and the health industry, healers, alternative practitioners, dietitians, and teachers.

Virgos are efficient, precise, analytical, critical, intro-verted, perfectionists. They have highly logical minds and find it hard to deal with illogical emotions. They are often kind, however, and will always give help when help is truly needed. When depleted, however, those born under this sign can become nervous, critical, cold, and sarcastic. It is more important for Virgos, than for nearly any other sign, to attend scrupulously to diet and hygiene. Virgos, being of a nervous disposition, must be sure to practice some form of relaxation or meditation. Being an earth sign, Virgos need to commune with nature on a regular basis.

Virgo the High Priestess has knowledge of health and healing and chooses to be of service to others. She symbolizes service, teaching, nurses, statisticians, analysts, draftsmen, designers—all areas that require either compassion and service to others, or well-developed attention to detail and a sense of perfection.

The High Priestess indicates a need for, or a desire to attempt, a balance among earthy and practical aspirations, intellectual reason and the emotions. It further indicates an active, intellectual mind capable of profound analysis and attention to detail. In other words, a reliable and conscientious worker. Virgos are the "workaholics" of the zodiac.

The High Priestess can indicate a need to reassess dietary and health regimes. A healthy interest in alternative medicine should be cultivated along with other fitness programs. Physical activity should emphasize improving the circulation. Virgos often work under stress and indoors, and this card highlights these issues.

TRADITIONAL INTERPRETATION

Wisdom. Common sense. Knowledge. Education. Penetration. Foresight. Intelligence. Comprehension.

COMMENTARY

The Tarot, Alfred Douglas: "In the tarot sequence the High Priestess is assigned the number two, which symbolizes counterpoise, relativity, the dualism that develops from the number one, or unity. It represents the interaction of poles which gives rise to manifestation and in the human sphere signifies mans experience of individual existence. It is the number of time, as opposed to timelessness, creation as opposed to creator, the reflected light of the Moon as opposed to the direct light of the sun." The caduceus can be seen as the poles to which Alfred Douglas refers. He continues, "Psychologically the High Priestess symbolizes one of the bridges linking the twin pillars of the conscious and unconscious minds, the inspirer of dreams and visions that reveal the continuance of life beyond conscious boundaries."

Royal Path to the Tarot, Joseph D'Agostino: "The key to the number two suggests duplication, duality, reflection, reversal, opposition, and production." Commenting on the Rider-Waite deck, he states, "The two pillars at her side are alike in shape and design, but different in color. Expounding the Hermetic principle of cause and effect these two pillars symbolically denote that all we experience is the collective reaction to mental patterns we consciously and unconsciously create."

3 The Empress/Libra ♎

A pyramid in the desert, with a tree growing beside it conveys female fertility, productivity, and creation.

ASTROLOGICAL INTERPRETATION

Libra is the seventh sign of the zodiac and represents a balancing point between the two halves of the zodiac. It also represents equality, judgment, balance, creativity, fertility, and justice.

Libras are often gentle and soft-spoken and can be extremely artistic. They have a profound sense of beauty.

Physiologically, Libra rules the kidneys which act as the body's "scales," balancing out every physical and emotional change experienced by the individual organism, such as hot and cold, happy and sad, and so on.

Libras therefore can be changeable, fickle, and fluctuate

like the scales, indecisive, argumentative, and superficial. However, they have a great need for companionship and partnership as a means to balancing themselves through others, and for this reason often marry young. Libra has a need for close relationships and is essentially self-expressive, communicative, and cooperative.

Due to its planetary ruler, Venus, Libra is a humanitarian sign with a love of harmony, beauty, and peace. Libras are often excellent artists and designers and may be involved in the legal professions at which they excel. They also make excellent diplomats.

Meanings for the Empress are: Creativity, fertility, femininity, and the power of visualization. Art, peace, harmony. Concord, fruitfulness, the feminine power of gestation. Love. Justice. Success. Accomplishment. Legal matters, lawsuits, or other legal contracts. Marriage, engagement, or birth, as well as partnership issues. Pregnancy or birth.

TRADITIONAL INTERPRETATION

Feminine progress. Action. Development. Fruitfulness. Fertility. Attainment. Accomplishment. Marriage. Material wealth.

COMMENTARY

Mastering the Tarot, Eden Gray: "Three is the number of the trinity, father, mother, and the son. The Empress expresses all that is meant by this fruitful union on the material plane. The Virgin High Priestess has now become the Earth Mother, the multiplier of images. The subconscious has developed the seed-thought planted in it, and now we have the material results."

The Tarot, Alfred Douglas: "The Empress is assigned the number three, the number of synthesis and harmony. It represents the resolving of the tension created by duality through the birth of a third unifying principle. Three is the number of childbirth, new life, fecundity and material productivity. The Empress is the great Mother Goddess, the source of all living things. She embodies the super-abundant creative forces of nature, together with the benign feminine wisdom of the queen of life. Her concerns are essentially those of the physical plane. She is the ruler of paradise on Earth....She is the descendant of earth goddesses such as the Greek Demeter or the Sumerian Ishtar, deities that probably preceded the masculine orientated pantheons of the classical worlds. They were the patronesses of Mystery cults such as that of Eleusis, at which the sacred dramas of death and the renewal of life were played out."

Jung and the Tarot, Sallie Nichols: "Generally speaking, the function of the number three is reflected in all sets of trinities. In all of these the third member acts as an equilibrating factor. An interesting correlation in this connection is that Pythagoras considered this number to be the first real number. The first two he said, were merely essences for they did not correspond to any geometric figure, thus they had no physical reality. But the number three creates the triangle, a plane surface with a beginning, a middle and an end." She continues, "I like to picture the Empress as the base of this triangle, for it is through her that the ephemeral is first brought within the realm of human experience."

4 The Emperor/Scorpio ♏

The yin-yang internalized in the pyramid was chosen to represent the internalizing functions of Scorpio, which rules this card. It represents hidden knowledge, the arcane, the profound and the mysteries.

ASTROLOGICAL INTERPRETATION

Scorpio is an intense, secretive, and powerful water sign. Ruled by Pluto, which governs sex and death, this is the first sign after the midway point of Libra and the first of the last six signs. The first six signs relate to personal awareness and development, and the latter to universal awareness and evolution. Scorpio then, has to plumb the depths of the mystical self without experience, and it is his destiny to uncover hidden truths, which will be developed in the remaining signs of the zodiac.

The typical Scorpio is sensitive to the extreme. Scorpios are psychic and deep, with a magnetic aura and powerful presence. The powers of deduction of this sign are legendary, as is its sexual prowess. The need for control and power, revenge and authority, are the downside of this sign, and a stubborn will and defensive attitude can alienate. The typical Scorpio can attract and alienate simultaneously. To their credit, and in my experience, Scorpios do not display the cruel side to their natures unless hurt or provoked. Be warned!

Scorpios (with their deadly ability to wait for revenge) make dangerous enemies, but their dedication, loyalty, and superb emotional control and love of mystery, make them good detectives, researchers, surgeons, military officers, and spies. If they use their higher power for good, as symbolized by the eagle associated with the sign, they can make dedicated healers and physicians.

In the same way that the legendary and mystical phoenix rises from the ashes, the typical Scorpio can regenerate his/her life by a series of transformations at a deep and meaningful psychic level. This allows him/her to intuitively eliminate old and outworn patterns or modes of existence, enabling the conscious self to re-establish a deeper rapport with the mystical self.

The Emperor symbolizes sex, sexuality, death, regeneration, emotional intensity, and transformation. It may also indicate inheritance and other people's resources. Physiologically it relates to the sexual organs.

TRADITIONAL INTERPRETATION

Worldly power. Accomplishment. Confidence. Wealth. Stability. Authority. Indomitable spirit. Aggressive.

COMMENTARY

The Tarot Speaks, Richard Gardner: "Life is ever moving and anything static is revolting to those with life. What you have of me will give you earthly wisdom in that area, but no authority to limit or brush aside vast areas you know nothing about. You can be as square as you like, so long as you do not force this shape upon others. My function is to establish and administer any knowledge gained from the heavens into the practical lives of men. . . . In truth I carry knowledge of both male and female powers and their respective forms of consciousness. When one knows of these, one knows of the enormous difficulties in reconciling them, and becomes aware that if it were not for Love, they could never be reconciled. Therefore a real hierophant is one who knows the nature of love and many secrets of lovemaking. As God is Love it is only he or she who knows the nature of Love that can truly pontificate."

The Tarot, Alfred Douglas: "The significance of the Emperor in the spiritual world is indicated by the device engraved on his throne or shield [relating to a deck designed by David Sheridan]. The eagle is said to symbolize the human soul purified by discipline and controlled willpower. Only by battling through the adversities of life and triumphing over circumstances can the spirit achieve freedom. In the Mundane world, the Emperor is he who by the intelligent use of his own resources has triumphed over physical restrictions. He has mastered the world around himself by constant effort and untiring tenacity."

Jung and the Tarot, Sallie Nichols: "Heretofore, we have been dealing with the primitive world of unconscious nature, now we step into the civilized world of conscious man. We leave the nonverbal, matriarchal realm of the Empress and here begins the patriarchal world of the creative word which initiates the masculine rule of spirit over nature."

5 *The High Priest/Jupiter* ♃

According to Vedic and Yogic literature and tradition, the kundalini energy (also known as life force or prana) is stored at the base of the spine in a pyramid form. The pyramid in this card reflects that fact and reminds us of ancient knowledge and wisdom.

The two columns represent the currents of energy that run up and down the spinal cord from the kundalini interconnecting the chakras. The columns are termed in Vedic literature as ida and pingala, yin and yang, positive and negative currents.

The purple sphere represents the awakening and rising of the kundalini expressed as spiritual wisdom, knowledge and enlightenment. It is associated with the third-eye center.

The color purple is ruled by Jupiter, the planetary ruler of this card. The two columns represent not only the alternating currents of ida and pingala, but also represent the astrological symbol for Gemini, the opposite to Sagittarius, which is ruled by Jupiter.

ASTROLOGICAL INTERPRETATION

In Greek mythology, Jupiter, or Zeus, was the biggest and greatest of the gods. In astronomical terms, Jupiter is the biggest of the planets. It rules the largest organ in the body, the liver. Jupiter also rules the hips and thighs, and it has a tendency to chest complaints through its polar opposite of Gemini.

Jupiter itself is composed mainly of silicates, and it is silica that composes the human eye. Quartz crystal contains vast amounts of silica. Under the microscope, silica molecules look like arrowheads, and the arrow is the symbol for Sagittarius. Jupiter can thus be said to rule the function of seeing in its spiritual sense, as in the awakened third-eye center, which sees beyond the physical.

Jupiter (The High Priest) is associated with the higher mind, higher education, spiritual expansion, and knowledge. It represents religion and philosophy and all religious and philosophical institutions. It governs expansion, both mental and physical, and has to do with long distance journeys and foreign lands.

Jupiter is expansive, jovial, capable of profound insights into the deeper, more spiritual aspects of life, and is essentially thoughtful, just, wise, magnanimous and generous, and is usually considered lucky.

On the negative side, Jupiter can cause restlessness, lack of attention to detail, boastfulness, scattering of energies, self-indulgence, excesses of behavior, and tactless speech.

Jupiter is also associated with the theater and has a propensity for performance through its co-rulership of Pisces. Jupiter (The High Priest) influences our spiritual attitudes and beliefs and is generally optimistic and expansive. There is a love of sports, outdoor activity, travel, debate, and an affinity of excitement and adventure.

TRADITIONAL INTERPRETATION

Kindness. Goodness. Inspiration. Compassion. A religious or spiritual leader. Can also be overgenerous and unconventional.

COMMENTARY

Tarot Classic, Stuart Kaplan: "The two columns in the card [referring to the Classic deck, but also present in the One World Tarot] represents duality, and whether or not we live within the law."

The columns, as we have already noted, represent the duality and choice afforded us in Gemini, and also represent the columns of energy that alternate within us: the positive and negative aspects of our own natures.

Once we ourselves become The High Priest, by opening and enlightening our higher minds with knowledge, with compassion and with faith, we can make positive choices and life directions. In essence, we are thus enabled to "aim" for a specific "target," again relating to the arrow of Sagittarius and its ability to aim and direct higher thought in an organized system of law and order.

At the end of the day, we all have choices (Gemini), but to make a good choice, we must employ moral and philosophical frameworks based on spiritual values (Sagittarius), as represented by The High Priest.

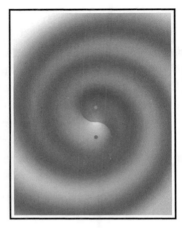

6 The Lovers/Venus ♀

The opposing forces of yin and yang combining and balancing into the yin-yang symbol represent a need for equilibrium and balance. Seen from a distance the image may also be seen as a sperm fertilizing an egg.

ASTROLOGICAL INTERPRETATION

Venus, long known as Aphrodite (the goddess of love) rules the signs of Taurus and Libra. Aphrodite comes from the word *fero*, which means, "to bear, bring forth, produce." Both Taurus and Libra are artistic, creative, and sensual. Venus represents unity through sympathy and feeling. Venus also rules the psychological function of judging and evaluating experience through the feelings, as opposed to logic.

Venus represents the feminine impulse in both sexes and is soft, passive, and receptive. Venus balances, harmonizes, resolves, unifies. She represents a need to appreciate and be appreciated. Venus is love, affection, and desire. Venus, above all, has a desire to unify opposites. Venus rules the throat area through Taurus, and the kidneys through Libra. The kidneys have the function of balancing all that we do, both physically and psychologically, as represented through the sign of Libra the Scales, which stands halfway in the twelve signs of the zodiac. In Libra, a balancing point between the two halves of the zodiac (yin-yang) must be reached for further development.

The Lovers represents love, duality, balance, beauty, fertility, creativity, artistic endeavors, legal matters, and further indicates a need for judgment. It indicates a need for a gentle, harmonious approach to matters, and it promises that situations will be resolved, provided a balanced and just harmony is achieved.

Negative traits are vanity, laziness, indecisiveness, fluctuation, superficiality, selfishness, procrastination, excess, imbalance, over-sensuous nature, self-indulgence, lack of commitment and fickleness.

TRADITIONAL INTERPRETATION

The necessity for testing, subjecting to trial. The struggle between the sacred and profane. Examining, speculating, tempting. Possible predicaments. Beauty. Compatibility. Harmony.

COMMENTARY

Tarot: The Royal Path to Wisdom, Joseph D'Agostino: "As you look [at this card], I am certain that you will be aware that what we have here is the allegorical story of the creation of man and woman. Here Adam, self-consciousness (yang) and Eve, subconsciousness (yin) enjoy the paradisiacal state. They are naked, free from all disguise. Can we experience this paradisiacal state of consciousness here on Earth? When woman is rightly understood, fully liberated from her subordinating role to Man, and returned to her proper place of equal status, then, the same Woman that took part in Mankind's fall from Paradise, will be instrumental in restoring Adam to his throne."

The Tarot, Alfred Douglas: "In psychological terms, Eros gives the capacity to relate opposing principles in a manner that not only harmonizes them but also results in a whole that is greater than its parts."

The Tarot: Path to Self Development, Micheline Stuart: "The trials of life have polished our roughness and transformed our violence. Our hearts are being filled with a vast love for the world and for humanity. True compassion, in its real sense, possesses us and love, in a higher, mature form, unlike the sentimental immature love on the earthy level, has entered us. Being no more imprisoned in nature, we are able to understand it in a new way, and at one with our surroundings, we have a marvelous appreciation of nature's beauty, its gifts and healing powers in our hearts." She continues, "As we are now in contact with our soul, we should allow it to be our guide, for its knowledge, perception and understanding are greater than ours. We are still but students of love, nevertheless, we are wide open to this warm and brilliant light. From the trials of life, we have learned the value of everything and know how useless it is to crave for more and more. . . . Love is the finest state, which a human can reach in his heart. The tremendous suffering and sorrow which mankind brings on itself are clearly seen and understood. Darkness is heavy and pulls us down, while lightness lifts us up into the luminous clarity of consciousness where things can be seen, apprehended, and loved."

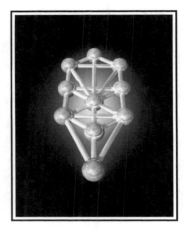

7 The Chariot/Sagittarius ♐

The Tree of Life here represents our spiritual side as represented by the philosophical sign of Sagittarius, which rules this card. Each Sephiroth represents a pathway we can choose in this life. Sagittarius represents the higher spiritual nature of someone who makes wise choices based on knowledge and insight into the divine workings of the creative.

The Chariot represents long distance travel, choices to be made, freedom, expansion, luck, wisdom, higher education, religion, and philosophy.

It is considered a "lucky" card in a reading and represents expansion, travel (both mental and physical) and opportunities.

ASTROLOGICAL INTERPRETATION

Sagittarius is the ninth sign of the zodiac, and is essentially expressive, energetic, adaptable, wise, just, and spiritual. Sagittarians are extremely expansive, philosophical and concerned with the "higher mind." They are enthusiastic, optimistic, sincere, and honest.

Sagittarius is ruled by Jupiter, the largest planet in the solar system, and Jupiter relates to the liver (the largest organ in the body), hips, and thighs. Sagittarius are open-minded, visionary, futuristic, intellectual, humorous, kind, open-hearted, frank, and outspoken.

On the negative side, this sign is extravagant, boastful, reckless, restless, careless, unreliable, over-optimistic, blunt, impatient.

Sagittarius, or those coming under the influence of this card, will be fortunate, talented, expansive, daring, and capable of great achievements—provided the restless nature is channeled into positive avenues. Often The Chariot indicates a variety of choices, and judgment being made on higher values and principles, as indicated by this expansive and philosophical sign.

TRADITIONAL INTERPRETATION

Ordeals, obstacles, effort, ascendancy, acclamation, conquest, victory, triumph, greatness. The determination to mix hard work with times of productive solitude.

COMMENTARY

Tarot: Path to Self Development, Michelene Stuart: "Now being in control of ourselves, we can take charge of the vehicle of our being and direct it through life, instead of it being tossed about by life, we have gained strength enough to harness the tremendous energies emitted by our worldly desires, by our animal passions, and by the forces of opposition. Once these are harnessed, they must be controlled from within our vehicle of being. . . . For purposes of higher development we have to guide ourselves through events, we know in what we are lacking and endeavor to remedy our deficiencies. No undertaking should remain neglected or only partly fulfilled. Life must no longer be our master, we must master life. The soul knows what we need and guides us to it. Our progress becomes a conscious process, our evolution becomes intelligent and our spirituality becomes active. At this stage, the soul, being in command, guides us to the throne of the spirit."

The Tarot, Alfred Douglas: "In the material world, the charioteer is he who has taught himself to control his bodily functions and concentrate all his faculties on a single goal. By the concentrated use of his trained intellect and his disciplined body, he rides confidently through the obstacles placed before him by circumstances, and dictates his own path. His practical understanding of the laws governing society give him the expertise to manipulate them to his own advantage."

The Chariot is the vehicle that will take us from Malkuth, materialized universe, to Kether the Crown, and beyond to En Soph, the limitless and boundless light.

Sagittarius has the need for spiritual knowledge and illumination, with his arrows pointing to heaven. He indicates that it is the path of wisdom and spirituality we must follow if we wish to transcend the material world and enter into the high realms of existence. With our Chariot, the incarnated body, firmly under our control, we may ascend the pathways from Malkuth (Earth) to heaven (En Soph), but we must remember to take one step at a time and carefully evaluate everything that stands between us and the infinite. It is a journey of many lifetimes. We need not rush. To make progress, wise actions must save us from our follies.

8 Justice/Capricorn ♑

The ouroboros (serpent eating its own tail) is a universal symbol that represents the totality, the eternal circle of disintegration and reintegration, the cyclic counterbalancing of opposing principles. It also represents self-sufficiency, perfect balance, strength, and endeavor.

The sphere at the center causes the image to resemble an eye, which represents the all-seeing divinity, enlightenment, illumination, and wisdom.

ASTROLOGICAL INTERPRETATION

Capricorn is the tenth sign of the zodiac and is ruled by the planet Saturn. It is the sign in which the year both ends and begins. Capricorn therefore represents both old age and youth.

This is the sign that is associated with the teeth, bones, and skeletal system—especially the knees—due to its Saturnian rulership.

Capricorns are cautious, ambitious, enterprising, practical, and introverted. They are patient, methodical, and resourceful, and are able to bear hardship and frustration. They are disciplined, self-contained and serious, prudent and conscientious.

Capricorns are plodding and patient, cautious and controlled.

Negative traits are depression, miserliness, aloofness, coldness, overly rigid attitude, extreme traditionalism, and indifference.

Saturn, which rules Capricorn, causes compression and densification (as opposed to expansion, which is ruled by Jupiter). Therefore, this card can indicate difficulties, delays, and restrictions. On the positive side, it can indicate the patience and perseverance required for success. Capricorn, like the mountain goat itself, will keep on climbing until reaching the summit.

TRADITIONAL INTERPRETATION

Justice symbolizes karma, justice, cyclic patterns, and return. It can indicate the ambition and drive needed for material success, and the ability to create foundations for business ventures and other enterprises.

Justice. Reasonableness. Moderation. Sensibility. Fairness. Poise. Virtue. Integrity. Honor. Self-satisfaction in accomplishments.

COMMENTARY

The Tarot, Alfred Douglas: "It [Justice] indicates the next stage in the life of the individual. He has reached maturity, finding his place in the world and achieving a secure environment. He has reaped the rewards of past efforts in terms of prosperity and status. He has reached the peak of success. But, in the moment of triumph, all is not as it should be, almost as if his life was missing some essential ingredient—Justice is the voice of conscience, the voice of the inner self. If the needs of the unconscious are suppressed, the conscious mind either becomes inflated, or often falls into profound depression. Only by accepting the challenge of the second half of life as eagerly as he accepted the first, can the sword of justice be avoided. Not that the challenge is one lightly met, the obstacles and perils of the inner way of the soul are equal to, if not greater than, those of the outer way of the World. In the mundane world Justice points the moral that we must all be weighed and receive our just desserts. If we would make the most of our destinies we must follow the rhythms of the universe or else be constantly beaten back.

Ignorance of the law is no more an excuse in the court of life than in the courts of men; the laws must be studied and obeyed if the penalties for transgressing them are to be avoided."

9 The Hermit/Aquarius ≈

Our Sun, four million light years away from its nearest relative, Alpha Centauri, is a hermit among the stars. It is alone in space, like the Hermit himself.

ASTROLOGICAL INTERPRETATION

Aquarius is the eleventh sign of the zodiac and is ruled by Uranus. Aquarius is associated with futuristic thinking, invention, genius, originality, science, electricity, technology. Aquarians are usually highly intelligent, intellectual, reforming, imaginative, and broadminded.

The negative traits of this sign are perversity, eccentricity, and fanaticism. Aquarius can be unconventional, rebellious, tactless, obsessive, detached, and erratic.

Aquarius rules the circulation (through a polarity with Leo) and governs the ankles. Aquarians therefore have a tendency to weak or sprained ankles and poor circulation.

Although Aquarians are friendly and gregarious, theirs is not a personal love, but more a love for all of humankind generally. They therefore do not always make ideal romantic partners, being more impersonal than personal.

Aquarians can be demanding, determined, fascinating people, independent, and fiercely frank, always one step ahead of the rest of us, somewhere in the future. When it is the moment that counts, Aquarians may be hard to pin down.

Their futuristic ideas make them great inventors, and they have a natural bent for electronics, technology, and computers.

TRADITIONAL INTERPRETATION

The Hermit symbolizes detachment, introspection, the time needed to incubate ideas. It can indicate a need to withdraw from the bustle of life, to think, plan and ponder, or may indicate enforced isolation.

Prudence. Deliberation. Inner wisdom. Caution. Circumspection. Self-denial. Withdrawal. Solicitude.

COMMENTARY

Tarot: The Path to Self Development, Michelene Stuart: "In modesty, without any illusion as to our knowledge, we realize how little we know in comparison with that of which we are ignorant. Here we are traveling into our own darkness, the subconscious. To have full knowledge of ourselves, it is as important to learn what is at the deepest interior levels as it is to learn about our exterior self and what lies on the surface. We have to work alone, protected from the external world. The higher truths we are learning must be hidden, for they are too powerful for people not prepared to hear them. It needs the long initiation of the way in order to become ready to bear them. Therefore we must remain silent. We must perform our daily tasks while sealing ourselves hermetically. Our aim requires us to concentrate our thoughts deeply if we are to reach the mystical and perfect equilibrium."

The Tarot, Alfred Douglas: "In some ways this card is analogous to the Fool. Here the seeker is again setting off on the first stage of a journey, alone, and with little to guide him. The feeble flickering of the inward light helps guide the Hermit on his way, it is his lantern, by the light of which he can discern a pathway before him. He illuminates the primeval darkness with the light of higher consciousness and drives away the shadows of the night."

Tarot: The Royal Path to Wisdom, Joseph D'Agostino: "The Hermit is a portrayal of the collective unconscious, the recorder and preserver of all manifestation, and the container of all potential possibilities available to man in any given age or time. The golden hexagram star [referring to the Rider-Waite deck] represents the solar light of the Spiritual Sun differentiated into the six universal forces. The Hermit elevates the magic lamp of light to guide us to the perfection he has attained. With love he watches over us as we tread the various paths upward. With compassion, he shares all our pains, our struggles and disappointments. Yet his inner voice speaks to the strong and the weak, urging us onward till we all scale the peak."

The Hermit is that part of ourselves that is connected to the whole universe, but still remains detached and alone. It is during these moments of profound silence that the truth speaks to us and through us, and by which flashes of insight are possible.

10 The Wheel of Fortune/Uranus ♅

The Wheel of Fortune, surrounded by the signs of the zodiac, can be likened to the wheel of birth and death. The Buddha himself levitates above The Wheel, demonstrating that he has achieved enlightenment and is beyond incarnation. This is signified by his illuminated third eye, or urna, "shining spot," "flaming pearl," and symbolizes unity, balance, and deliverance from the world of duality.

ASTROLOGICAL INTERPRETATION

Uranus represents impersonal drives and ambitions and is said to rule electricity and technology, the Aquarian Age, insight and inspiration, sudden unexpected events, and groups and societies. Uranus rules Aquarius. Uranus also rules the unusual and the unpredictable, and has an effect on genius, with a special bent for invention and innovation.

The Wheel of Fortune can be said to rule inspiration, sudden flashes of insight, sudden and unexpected changes, the unusual, the unconventional and the innovative, and has association with clubs, groups and societies, music technology, computers, electricians and electrical engineers, and all those in allied areas. It can also indicate an inspired thinker and inventor.

The negative virtues of this energy can be self-willed, rigid, inflexible, dictatorial, contrary, eccentric, and intense. With his propensity for the totally unexpected, Uranus, The Wheel of Fortune, can bring chaos and the unexpected, electrical storms, explosions, sudden earthquakes, and so on.

The Wheel tells us that beyond form and incarnation is the pure energy of life. While we have desires and return to incarnate, we shall be subject to the changes of destiny as dictated by our fate.

The Wheel in essence warns us that wise decisions must be made so as not to tempt the fates with sudden and impulsive actions. We are reminded that our actions will come back to us on the wheel of birth and death in a never ending cycle, until perfection is reached.

TRADITIONAL INTERPRETATION

Fate, destiny, fortune. Unexpected events. One must be alert to unexpected opportunity.

COMMENTARY

The Tarot: Path to Self Development, Micheline Stuart: "In a state of detachment, The Wheel of eternal recurrence which brings the ups and downs of everyday life can be watched. Never for a moment does the cosmic wheel stay still. We are carried on it in perpetual motion. Without a supreme effort to detach ourselves from it [as symbolized by the Buddha who remains above the Wheel itself] we remain on this [wheel], ever at its mercy. . . On attaining control of our passions and desires, the turning wheel bringing its good or bad opportunities can be watched objectively. By now we have gained a certain ability to discriminate and to be alert to recognize and seize the opportunity offered in each present moment. But we must be swift to act, for opportunities pass quickly. It is a state of understanding, of valuation. We are strong enough now to take the initiative for higher purpose."

The Tarot, Paul Foster Case: "The Wheel is the symbol of the whole cycle of cosmic expression, and is also an emblem of any particular series of events. The Wheel itself combines the ideas of rotation, cycles, ascent, and descent. The Wheel, moreover is a symbol of progress, advancement and improvement."

Mastering the Tarot, Eden Gray: "The Wheel of Fortune keeps on turning and carries men and their destinies up and then down. Spiritual reality is unchanging, but the wheel of personal life turns."

The Tarot, Alfred Douglas: "The Wheel is a mandala, a symbol of psychic wholeness and inner order. The hub of the wheel is the still mystic center, surrounded by the radiating paths that lead to the self."

The Wheel reminds us that life is power and energy. It deals fairly with all. It is we who create our destinies by our very actions. We must continue the struggle for ultimate spiritual purity, which we will finally attain (cyclically speaking) in the sign of Pisces, the last of the zodiac and the last sign on our evolutionary journeys.

The Wheel reminds us that we must expect the unexpected and must remain alert at all times.

11 Strength/Neptune ♆

The all-seeing eye represents the third eye, which indicates spiritual knowledge and wisdom. The pyramid represents arcane knowledge, and the sea above which the pyramid floats represents the unconscious, emotional, or spiritual plane.

ASTROLOGICAL INTERPRETATION

Neptune represents the human psyche's potential for individual mystical self-realization (mind or evolving spirit) and the transcending of the physical and material planes of consciousness.

Neptune is magical and mystical and defines the power of our creative visualization and imagination through identification with the source. The powerful influence of Neptune on the unconscious mind imbues it with great powers of visualization, imagination, and creativity, coupled with a great psychic sensitivity.

Neptune, which rules Pisces, confers great tenderness of feeling, receptivity, mediumistic and clairvoyant powers and a sensitivity to beauty, music, and art.

This card symbolizes great creative power in art, music, poetry, and the performing arts. Those with a strong Neptunian influence are in tune with the world beyond form and are able to commune with it, whereby they are inspired by visions, dreams and revelations normally beyond the confines of the conscious mind.

Strength is spiritual strength in as much as the vibrations of Neptune enable us to perceive the magical, mystical, and supernatural in creation for all its glory. It is the transcendental experience—it is the realization of God. It therefore has associations with religion, churches, places of healing or worship, and the sea.

The negative traits are self-delusion, escapism, lack of direction, psychological confusion, and drug and alcohol abuse.

TRADITIONAL INTERPRETATION

Strength. Courage. Accomplishment. Innate ability. Zeal. Mind over matter. Conquest. Hidden forces. Triumph of love. Liberation.

COMMENTARY

Understanding the Tarot, Jocelyn Almond and Keith Seddon: "The traditional image is either Hercules wrestling with the Nemean lion or a woman taming a lion. The Hercules version seems to denote physical strength, when in fact, it is moral strength and self-control, which is represented here. . . . In a well-balanced personality, the energy of these emotions is channeled into creative and positive activity, so that it becomes a source of strength."

The strength of this card refers to inner spiritual powers and energies that we must both understand and control if we are to benefit from them.

Jung and the Tarot, Sallie Nichols: "When human consciousness recognizes and accepts its untamed, primitive nature, it not only frees itself from the instinct's autonomous power, but liberates and transforms the instinctual side as well."

Neptune will inspire us but we must respect his power. Richard Gardner writes of Strength in *The Tarot Speaks*: "I am the Enchantress often known as La Force because I am the greatest power on Earth. It was my power that built that civilization you all now pretend did not exist. This denial of me comes from your terror, not your intelligence, for you were so pleased with my wondrous powers that you grew me in you out of balance until I brought the flood upon your heads, because my power is based in the magic dynamic of water. How many of you can even imagine a civilization based on a totally different power source? Yet it existed and some of you are now beginning to rediscover its trace. In all official religious teachings ref-

erence to me has been eliminated in favor of solely patriarchal doctrines. . . . What operates me is that blue
dynamic you can see in the sky all around the Earth. In
the days of Atlantis you knew my secrets and lived upon
my powers and all was done by charm. I am still with you,
for intellect ever follows the imagination."

12 *The Hanging Man/Pisces* ♓

Everything is upside down, and instead of ascending, we descend.

ASTROLOGICAL INTERPRETATION

Pisces is the last sign of the zodiac in which the human soul can incarnate. It represents a completion of the cycle, the circle of life. Having come from the spiritual realms, we must now leave the world of matter behind us and embark on the next step of our great spiritual journey.

Pisces people, therefore, are often sensitive, compassionate, spiritual, and non-materialistic. They have an affinity with artists, actors, performers, hospitals, nurses, and institutions.

As this card is the inverse of the preceding card, it implies the negative aspects of this sign, which can be manifested as confusion, alcohol and drug addiction, mental illness or breakdown, self-delusion, self-escapism through drugs, fantasy, illusion, and further indicates a lack of definition between the two halves of the brain and an overemphasis on the use of the right brain. It indicates someone who has lost definition in life, someone who is confused, lacking direction, and lacking an ability to apply logic. Thus they respond to situations from a purely emotional vantage point.

The Hanged Man card suggests a need to balance out the intuition and sensitivity with discipline and logic and may further suggest that the querent has become so subjective that he/she has lost all objective powers of reasoning and sees the world as if it were upside down. This person needs grounding. An excess of the emotional water element must be constructively channeled if it is not to take the psyche further downward in a spiral of self-pity and self-delusion.

TRADITIONAL INTERPRETATION

Life in suspension. Reversal of the mind and one's way of life. Transition. Abandonment. Sacrifice. Readjustment. Regeneration. Rebirth.

COMMENTARY

Tarot Classic, Stuart Kaplan: "We see in The Hanged Man the moment of suspension at which truth and realization are revealed. The cloak of secrecy is removed. The inner self is exposed. Although the man is still earthbound, he has attained in his fashion some measure of relief through the suspension and transition of his life. The events of the past are mesmerized in the present calm before the cascade of the future, which lies in wait ahead. Repentance is the present salvation."

And perhaps it is the only salvation, for as Sallie Nichols writes in *Jung and the Tarot*: "The Hanged Man is as helpless as a turnip. He is in the grasp of Fate. He has no power to shape his life or control his destiny. Like a vegetable, he can only wait for a force outside himself to pluck him free from the regressive pull of Mother Earth."

Alfred Douglas is quite emphatic about the Hanged Man and writes in *The Tarot*: "He is aware that he is not one person, the conscious self he identifies with, but only part of a greater whole. He sees two halves which are antagonistic to one another, yet are at the same time complementary." [This is reflected in the symbol for Pisces, the two fish swimming in opposite directions.] "He realizes that in casting himself off from the solid ground of his past consciousness, he can only trust that a larger power will support him and stop him falling into a psychic void. In order to proceed he must have the courage to let go of all he has learnt, voluntarily release the grip of the intellect and allow the deeper forces within to take the reins. To deliberately float oneself on the secret tides of the unconscious implies a deliberate reversal of the teachings and values of the outer world, and the acceptance of a grave risk. The laws and values of the inner worlds are in many cases the exact reverse of those we are familiar with, and are only transgressed at one's peril."

Failure to find the vital balance between consciousness and unconsciousness will inevitably result in personal confusion and chaos that the Hanged Man, precariously positioned as he already is, can ill afford.

13 The Rebirth/Aries ♈

The Shri Yantra, a circle full of concentric triangles, is
the pattern made by sound when Om, written in the
center, is recited. Om is said to be the sound that first
brought the material universe into manifestation, and
therefore here it symbolizes the beginning of all things.

ASTROLOGICAL INTERPRETATION

Aries is the first sign of the zodiac. It symbolizes new
beginnings, new cycles, and the beginning of a new astrological year. Aries is said to rule the head and brain. Aries
must also have the dynamic power to initialize the rebirth
of the cycles of nature after the end of winter.

Aries begins on the spring equinox (March 21st) when
growth begins anew, and Aries people inherit the same
dynamic energy, which makes them excellent leaders and

organizers. Aries are the pioneers of the zodiac. They inspire and initiate. Through their brave spirits and tireless and boundless energy they are able to creatively visualize and organize new projects.

Aries are honest, direct, and forthright. They are usually entertaining, lively and enthusiastic, open, friendly, and sincere.

On the negative side, Aries people, or those under an Aries influence, can be selfish, self-centered, egotistical, childish, impatient, ill-tempered, dictatorial, arrogant, aggressive, and bullying.

Formerly known as the Death card, the Rebirth card reminds us that in life, at a spiritual and cellular level, nothing ever actually dies, but is transformed and reborn. This card therefore signifies the ending of situations, cycles, or relationships—but with this ending a new beginning is promised.

The Rebirth further symbolizes new beginnings, new opportunities, change, renewal, revival, and reanimation.

TRADITIONAL INTERPRETATION

Transformation. Alteration. Sudden change. Great change. Death of the old self, though not necessarily physical death. End or loss. The beginning of a new era.

COMMENTARY

The Tarot: Key to the Wisdom of the Ages, Paul Foster Case: "Nun (the Hebrew letter with which this card is associated) as a verb means 'to sprout, to grow.' The essential idea is fertility, fecundity, productiveness, generative power. Motion is the function attributed by Kabbalists to Nun, and from this are derived a great variety of other meanings such as 'to grow.'"

Spring and the beginning of Aries is the very time when nature starts to reproduce and grow.

Tarot Classic, Stuart Kaplan: "The card of [Death] represents the transitional phenomena of decay and death modified to rebirth and reincarnation. The finality of the past is removed from the future through the irrevocable sweep of the scythe [referring to a traditional deck]. The fear of change often overshadows the promise of new direction and the opportunities, which await the person capable of altering the course of his life's direction. The reaper sweeps away the weeds symbolic of the confining conditions surrounding him [referring to the traditional image of the grim reaper] and the rebirth and regeneration begins almost immediately."

All endings must be followed by new beginnings. This universal law of nature is at work in our everyday lives. As Alfred Douglas puts it in *The Tarot:* "The Arabic number thirteen is made up of the numbers one and three and is therefore analogous to the number four as a symbol of order and organization. Death, though apparently the agent of chaos, is in fact the instigator of a new order which follows life." He continues, "The mundane explanation of this card says that death is the principle of nature which sweeps away old life and clears the ground for the growth of the new. Without death, life could hardly have begun, but death is not the end: old life not only makes way for new, but also supplies the material for its structure. The future springs from the rich loam of the past. Nothing is lost and nothing is wasted, only the form changes."

14 Temperance/Taurus ♉

The symbol for pi, constructed as the pillars of Stonehenge, symbolizes sacred mathematical science, construction, building, form, solidity, and security. It also represents material and physical laws that operate on the earth plane.

ASTROLOGICAL INTERPRETATION

Taurus is the second sign of the zodiac. Taurus creates the structure required for the materialization and maintenance of material form.

Taurus rules all those things needed to maintain the self: food, housing, shelter, clothing, and personal possessions including finances, wealth, and property.

As Taurus is ruled by Venus, it also produces fine artists, dancers, and craftspeople. These people can also make excellent antiques dealers, property dealers, builders and tradespersons, and have associations with land and property. Taurus people often attract wealth and have a hefty appetite for all things material and sensual.

On the negative side, Taurus can be lazy, stubborn, insensitive, greedy, grasping, and self-indulgent. Taurus can be the proverbial "bull in a china shop."

Physiologically, Taurus rules the throat area and the thyroid, which can impact weight control in the body. Due to their love of rich food and their disregard for physical exercise, Taureans are prone to put on weight.

Temperance symbolizes wealth, material success and material possessions, and can indicate matters involving property, housing, and the home. It also indicates a need to stabilize and to develop a solid base from which the self can operate.

TRADITIONAL INTERPRETATION

Moderation. Patience. That which can be accomplished through self-control and frugality. Harmony. Fortunate omen. Consolidation. Ability to recognize and utilize the material manifestations available to oneself.

COMMENTARY

Tarot: The Path to Self Development, Michelene Stuart: "Hitherto we were ruled by the laws of accident, anything could happen to us at any time, as is the lot of sleeping humanity. Now we are under a different law, that which governs our real being, our essence. Our guardian angel is starting to protect us: it is he who pours the divine fluid, the vital force into our newly cleansed vessel."

The Tarot: Key to the Wisdom of the Ages, Paul Foster Case: "Samech [the Hebrew letter for this card] means 'tent peg' or 'prop.' It is what makes a tent secure, and thus corresponds to what would now be suggested to us by the foundation of a house. It is therefore the letter symbol of that which is the basis or support of our house of life. It is that which sustains, preserves and maintains our personal existence."

Our form was created at the beginning (Aries). Now Taurus will supply the form with all its material needs.

The Tarot, Alfred Douglas: "The word temperance in this context is meant in the old sense of the mixing of ingredients in the right proportion. This card is therefore emblematic of the conjunction of opposites. It is assigned the number fourteen, which in Arabic numerals is made up of the numbers one and four. The combination of unity and the quaternary produces the pentagon, the five-sided figure, illustrating organic growth, inspiration and the reconciliation of several parts into a greater whole."

Understanding the Tarot, Jocelyn Almond and Keith Seddon: "Temperance in this sense refers to the practice of tempering something by mixing other substances with it. Temperance is finding the right balance or mixture, and refers to alchemical practices in which one tries to transform base metal into gold, a symbol for perfecting the self and raising it to a higher spiritual level."

The Tarot Speaks, Richard Gardner: "I am Temperance, Time, the great alchemist. Through me all comes to fruition and every form finds its ultimate destiny. I transform that which is base and low to the highest quality it can reach. Work with me and become wonderful."

15 Deliverance/Saturn ♄

Saturn rules the sign of Capricorn. The winter solstice occurs on December 21st, when the solar day is shortest, and night longest. The time ruled by Saturn is midwinter, the darkest hours of the year. The Sun is obscured by the planet Saturn. The light of the Sun is at its weakest and darkness dominates.

ASTROLOGICAL INTERPRETATION

Saturn is often identified with Kronos, the Greek god of time, and is often depicted as the reaper, the timekeeper with hourglass and scythe, the symbol of the limit of life—which must inevitably end with death. These human boundaries are symbolized by Saturn's rings. Saturn represents the boundaries that regulate and control growth. He rules form and structure, crystallization and constriction, and the skeleton, teeth, and bones.

Deliverance suggests delays, restrictions, a need for discipline and a planned course of action. It can indicate success through hard work and perseverance, or can indicate failure due to restrictions.

At its best this influence can promise success, but not without effort, toil, and patience. It may also indicate a depressive and overly serious personality, mean both with affection and with material displays of generosity. Saturn limits, constricts, constrains, delays, and adds a serious note to whatever venture with which it is associated.

For those under Saturn's influence, hard work, hardship, depression, and an introverted, cautious personality may be restrictive factors. However, those who can cultivate an optimistic frame of mind, and who find a disciplined framework for their lives, may eventually achieve success by reaching the top of the mountain in slow and deliberate moves when others have long since given up.

When we are engrossed in the materialism of Saturn, we lose our light and become enslaved to the material world, forgetting our divinity. (It is interesting to note that this card has always been known as The Devil card, the Devil being another name for Satan. Satan is a derivation of the word Saturn.)

The darkness associated with the winter solstice is symbolic of our darkest selves, the proverbial devil within us all. This card is renamed Deliverance, as the light is always there to guide us home. In our darkest hours and moments all may seem lost, but the seed of love and light remains.

TRADITIONAL INTERPRETATION

Subordination, bondage, malevolence, subservience, downfall. Lack of success. Unexpected failure. Seeming inability to realize one's goals. Dependence. Self-punishment. Temptation. Ill-temper. Lack of humor.

COMMENTARY

The Tarot, Alfred Douglas: "Here we have another card concerned with the reconciliation of consciousness with unconscious elements. Having forged a link with his inner self, the seeker is now able to proceed further in search of the hidden center. He is no longer isolated inside the narrow confines of his ego but has established contact with the creative forces of the unconscious. It is at this stage that he first encounters the powerful figures, which are not simply part of his personal psyche, but belong to the unconscious strata of humanity as a whole. These are the primordial images, which belong to the dawn of existence, the othonic gods whose power is vast and who hold a deadly attraction for the conscious mind. The collective unconscious, like the ego, has a shadow side that contains all the unrealized aspects of mankind. In Christianity this is personified as Satan, The Devil, the great tempter."

"In the ancient world," he continues, "this untamed force was embodied in such deities as Dionysus of whom

Jung has said, 'Dionysus is the abyss of impassioned dis-
solution, where all human distinctions are merged in the
animal divinity of the primordial psyche—a blissful and
terrible experience.'"

If the challenge of the collective shadow can be met
and recognized for what it is, and brought within the
sphere of consciousness in a measured and controlled
manner, then the forces of darkness may be transformed
into the power of light. In the darkness of death lie the
seeds of new life. Thenceforth, Saturn, ruler of the dark,
becomes Lucifer, the shining angel whose name means
"The Light Bringer."

16 The Tower/Mars ♂

The tower represents the human body, and the red sphere symbolizes the head, which Aries rules. The lightning represents disruption, danger, the unexpected, and unforeseen.

ASTROLOGICAL INTERPRETATION

Mars rules Aries and Scorpio. The color of Mars is red. Arians under the strong influence of Mars are bold, assertive, impulsive, reckless, and impatient. They tend to do things in the heat of the moment. The Tower warns that impatience and impulsive behavior could lead to unforeseen reactions and situations. It emphasizes a need for careful thought and planning and a balanced judgment system.

Mars, traditionally the god of war, is strong, daring and brave, but can also be violent and cruel—qualities shared by Scorpio whom Mars co-rules with Pluto. Mars also relates to the physical aspect of sex, desire, passion, and lust. He rules the head through his association with Aries, and sexuality through his rulership of Scorpio.

The Tower warns of hasty, impulsive actions. It warns against force, oppression, dominance, and control. It can indicate quarrels, violence, aggression and arrogance, and hasty, ill-conceived actions. Energy and enthusiasm cannot exist successfully without moral structure careful planning and cool judgment. Act now/think later, and "rushing in where fools fear to tread" is typical of those under this influence. To work successfully with strong, powerful Martian energy careful analysis of situations should be made. Dangerous if unleashed without wisdom, Martian energy should be used carefully and wisely so as not to mishap upon oneself or others.

Cultivating an awareness of cause and effect and curbing rash behavior with well thought-out planning can make the powerful energy positive. The Tower remains a strong warning that if our actions are hasty, ill-conceived, and without solid foundation, they will bear the same fruits.

TRADITIONAL INTERPRETATION

Unexpected events. Disruption. Adversity. Calamity. Downfall. Undoing. Ruin. Loss of stability.

COMMENTARY

The Tarot, Alfred Douglas: "The top of the tower is seen to have been struck off by a fiery bolt from heaven. Symbolically the crown of an edifice frequently represents the peak of consciousness, revealing that in its flashing descent the lightning of pure selfhood, the primal energy of the psyche strikes aside and rends all structures of the ego."

"Human consciousness here is at last in direct contact with the primary forces of the hidden center, the goal of the mystic quest. The light of Lucifer is not the gentle radiance of intuition filtering up from the depths, but the full glare of God consciousness, undimmed light such as blinded Paul on the road to Damascus."

Ego is our individualized idea of self, which is embodied in the first sign of Aries as we begin the cycle of evolution. Ego is who we think we are. Spirit is who we are. When we act from the spirit, which is pure, our actions succeed. When we operate from an inflated sense of self-importance our actions are often doomed to fail.

How to Foretell your Future in the Cards, Kathleen McCormack: "The origin of this card is thought to lie in the rites of the Dionysian cult which was linked with Mithras. The Titans tore Dionysus to pieces and were blasted by divine lightning, then Dionysus arose like the Phoenix reborn from the ashes in the new personality of Iacchus. The same force which destroyed the Titans regenerated Dionysus. The power of enlightened good has defeated the power of ignorance and evil, or winter is dead, a world is reborn, a new god arises."

Mars rules Aries, which is the first sign of spring. Symbolically, Mars has the energy to commence the cycle of life anew, but with wisdom and firm foundations he must act or all will come to naught.

17 The Star/Gemini Ⅱ

The Star of David represents knowledge, wisdom and the Law of Moses. The six-pointed star represents the complementary opposites of spirit and matter. Being composed of two triangles, one inverted, and one on its base, it represents the intertwining of opposites into manifested creation, like the symbol used in ancient China to denote yin and yang. Matter and spirit joined in ceaseless interaction is experienced through the conscious and the unconscious alike.

ASTROLOGICAL INTERPRETATION

Gemini is an intellectual air sign, the symbol for which is the twins. Like our brain, which is both conscious and unconscious and composed of two halves, the typical Gemini is always in "two minds."

The typical Gemini can view any process or sequence of events logically and unemotionally. Gemini is ruled by Mercury and is therefore intellectual, inquisitive, social, gregarious, communicative, talkative, self-expressive, with a keen mind and sharp wit. Gemini is also extremely intellectually restless, has a love of change and variety, and is mentally active and adaptable.

Gemini rules the shoulders, arms, hands, and lungs. It also rules the nervous system. Many Geminis make excellent singers, lecturers, and teachers and they are usually good at language, which is essential to express their keen communication skills.

The negative traits of this sign are superficiality, changeableness, unreliability, coldness, two-facedness, fickleness, inconsistency, and cunning. The natives under this influence are nervous and high strung, and they resent restrictions of any sort, their freedom being paramount.

Gemini rules short-distance journeys, journeys by air, brothers, sisters, and neighbors. The Star also symbolizes intellectual capacity and indicates talents in journalism, language, writing, and communication skills. Anyone under this influence is alert, requiring much information to fuel an inquiring and inquisitive mind. Variety and change are important under this influence. It is therefore all the more important to cultivate and define focused goals.

TRADITIONAL INTERPRETATION

Hope, faith, inspiration, bright prospects. Knowledge, fulfillment, satisfaction, desire, work, hope, and effort.

COMMENTARY

Tarot: The Royal Path to Wisdom, Joseph D'Agostino: "Having equipped ourselves with reliable knowledge, we focus our consciousness by an act of attention on a selected point of inquiry and hold it there. This single occupation of consciousness seals our senses from outer distraction, re-directing them inwardly. The gradual descent into the depths of the mind stirs the unconscious into action, attracting all relevant images directly associated with our central thought. As we mentally follow this unbroken flow of images, we eventually arrive at its very essence. Here we observe the seed idea in its pristine state, free from distortions fabricated by the misinterpretations of personality. Elaborations of these illuminating perceptions induce adjustments in personality which, in effect, synchronize a portion of our consciousness with the universal principles."

The Tarot Speaks, Richard Gardner: "I am the Star of Hope. I am always here to give you another chance when the edifice you have built collapses. Sometimes you see this as an irrevocable tragedy, but where you have more spirit you see it as freeing you from the all too many restrictions and injustices that it had created. We must always go on, is the rule of life. Not to wallow in what was

lost, or be vilified by others when we know that all endings are chances of new beginnings. To give up is to die.
Life is inexorable and will have its way. Bear this in mind
and expect little sympathy or help from fate when you
have given up. I am the great aim, that towards which all
functions work to fulfill themselves. And so long as you
allow life on your planet I shall be here drawing you
towards your true destiny individually and universally."

He continues, "There is really no such thing as a person not knowing what his true vocation is. When a person is lost, it arises from living in a time that denies much
of that person's soul and its potential. Look well into
yourself and accept all you find there irrespective of the
opinions of your time about it. Then you will find the
inner spark of life from which you will find direction."

18 The Moon/Cancer ♋

The Moon is just after new. Most of its form is hidden by the shadow of the Earth, with just a little light shed on its surface. The Moon represents the unconscious, feminine side of our natures, as opposed to the conscious, male energies of the solar light. Here, just a little light shines on our unconscious. New ideas are forming but they are yet in their infancy. Much is still veiled in mystery.

ASTROLOGICAL INTERPRETATION

Cancer is a water sign and is ruled by the Moon. Those under its influence are extremely sensitive psychically and emotionally, and have a deep need for emotional security. There is a deep love of home and family and a special fondness for children. This sign is said to rule the "mothering instinct" in both men and women, and Cancerian men may be the most family-oriented of the entire zodiac.

Cancerians can be introverted, shy, and insecure with a tendency to dwell on past hurts, or to retreat into their "shell" when they are wounded or threatened. This sign also relates to the past, to history and to family heritage, and Cancerians must attempt to let go of the past if they are to move forward.

Physiologically, Cancer rules the stomach and breasts. If the emotions are in turmoil, stomach problems will be the result.

The Moon can represent the unconscious drives, the emotions, the mother, and the nurturing principle.

Cancerians, ruled by the Moon, are usually sympathetic, sensitive, and intuitive but can be self-repressing and passive. Due to its tendency to hold on to things, Cancer the Crab can be overly cautious with money, and very security conscious. They can hold on to emotional hurts in the same way. Like the Crab who walks sideways, Cancerians tend to side-step issues and do not usually employ direct methods in their actions and relationships. They can be overly sentimental, easily hurt, and vulnerable emotionally.

TRADITIONAL INTERPRETATION

The Moon implies deception. Trickery. Insincerity. Dishonesty. Double-dealing. Deceit. Craftiness. That which comes out of the deep and unknown.

COMMENTARY

Tarot Classic, Stuart Kaplan: "The Moon triumphs over the stars because it is brighter and closer to Earth. . . The Moon demonstrates its power over the water and Man is torn between many influences."

The emotional life of man is dominated by the many phases of the Moon. The Moon in our card is barely lit. Much of it lies in darkness, unseen. The unconscious has but a small light upon it. We must be aware of our unconscious and emotional responses to situations if we are to avoid self-deception and illusion.

Eden Gray, in *Mastering the Tarot*, describes the Moon as representing "unforeseen perils, deception, change. Intuition, and the unfoldment of latent powers. In its highest sense, the Moon is the keeper of the mysteries of the universe."

The Sun represents our conscious awareness, but the Moon emphasizes that which is embryonic and unseen. Alfred Douglas writes in *The Tarot*: "The Moon was anciently believed to be the abode of the Dead. The souls of the dying would leave their bodies and be drawn silently up into the Moon. There they would be kept safe until the time of rebirth. The Moon symbolized the maternal womb, which was the giver of new life. Thus the Moon had a dual aspect: it was feared as the dark cavern of death, and revered as the portal into new life."

19 The Sun/Leo ♌

The Sun is the center of our solar system. Without the Sun's rays, there would be no life. The Sun card symbolizes energy, power, a need to be the "center," the need to radiate, project, and shine.

ASTROLOGICAL INTERPRETATION

Leo is ruled by the Sun. Thus, those born under the influence of the Lion take on characteristics of the Sun itself.

Leos love to shine, to be the center of attention, and they can be very creative. They are particularly attracted to show business, where their ability to hold a crowd makes them popular and successful performers.

Leos can also be arrogant, self-centered, vain, and boastful. They can be proud and assertive, overbearing and dominating.

On the positive side, they can be generous, warm-hearted, enthusiastic, dignified, and dramatic. They can have a need to attain positions of authority and make good organizers. Leos are self-expressive, energetic and assertive, with qualities of intensity and determination.

Leo rules the heart, the center of the body around which all the other organs exist. It is from the heart that the blood is pumped all around the body, thus supplying all the other organs with the blood they need. In much the same way, the Sun pumps out light and energy for all the planets. Leo also rules the heart in an emotional sense, and influences love affairs and creativity. Those ruled by the Sun must remember, however, that the Sun (consciousness, male) shines on us for only half the day. During the other half, the night, it is the Moon (unconsciousness, female) who has dominion.

TRADITIONAL INTERPRETATION

Satisfaction. Accomplishment. Contentment. Success. Triumph. Comfort. Pleasure. Rewards. Material wealth. Love. Joy.

COMMENTARY

According to Eileen McCormack in *Tarot: How to Foretell Your Future in the Cards*: the Sun is "The celestial master to the initiate in the mysteries, to the ordinary person, the Sun brings warmth, joy, laughter and abundance. The ancient talisman for success showed a crowned king. To many of the ancients, the Sun was a symbol of kingship and royalty." She further adds that the Sun represents strength and courage.

It is no coincidence that the talisman for success should be a golden crown. Gold itself is ruled by Leo and represents wealth and worldly power. Leo is also associated with royalty and monarchy, and sun spot activity was recently found to coincide with the rise and fall of great civilizations.

In *Jung and the Tarot*, Sallie Nichols says: "The Sun is the source of all life on this planet. We receive energy directly from its rays. Many people, notably the Egyptians, the Aztecs, and the American Indians, have worshipped the Sun as the supreme Creator."

Joseph D'Agostino writes in *Tarot: The Royal Path to Wisdom:* "The Sun is a symbol of our individuality. This focus of solar energy creates what psychology terms the 'ego.' Based on the moment of birth the angle of the Sun, in conjunction with the positions of the other planets, form the patterns which determine the structure of the grosser vehicles which we refer to as our personality and physical body."

The Tarot: Path to Self Development, Michelene Stuart: "We have to reassess and change our values if we are to surmount our animal nature. Only then can we begin to discern the clear spirit of our aim. Being still young we are vulnerable to the wiles of the ego, which will seek to appropriate our zealousness for itself, to bolster is existence. The forces of opposition are centered in our ego, giving rise to the strongest yet entirely fictitious conviction that we are truly ourselves, thus constituting an implacable enemy to our essential selves. Only by seeing ego for what it is can its powers be diminished, and only by the growth of consciousness can we begin to realize that which is truly ourselves is of another order of being."

20 The Judgment/Moon ☽

The full Moon symbolizes illumination, light shining on that which was hidden. It is the unconscious illuminated and secret knowledge revealed. The Moon totally illuminated reveals to us inner truths and points the way to the sacred self, which usually remains unseen.

ASTROLOGICAL INTERPRETATION

The Moon is known to govern the tides. The Moon also governs the menstrual and fertile cycles of all life forms. The symbol for the Moon, the incomplete circle, represents the mind, the evolving human spirit, and the dual nature of life—part conscious and part unconscious.

The Moon is the Earth's satellite but the Sun is still the center of gravity for both bodies. The Earth-Moon system is, in effect, a double planet. This suggests the dual nature of the Moon, divided between the pull of the Sun (spirit) and Earth (physical body).

The Moon represents our emotions and our unconscious drives and defines the condition of our feminine side. The Moon also rules the digestive system, stomach, breasts, and menstrual and fertility cycles. The Moon establishes an essential rhythm in the body and instinctive mind. The Moon is also associated with past and present and the deepest associations with one's family and ancestors through the mother. The Moon is the astrological ruler of Cancer and rules the fourth house.

The Judgment can be said to rule our processes at the deepest and most unconscious level. That which is suppressed or dormant will be made available to our conscious mind.

The Judgment tells us that all our actions are recorded on our unconscious minds. For example, under hypnosis people can recall the smallest detail at any moment in time. All things will be made visible, and nothing is forgotten.

TRADITIONAL INTERPRETATION

Atonement. Judgment. The need to repent and forgive.
Accountability. Rebirth. Improvement. The day of judgment has arrived. The evaluation of one's efforts and
accomplishments may be near at hand.

COMMENTARY

Tarot: The Path to Self Development, Micheline Stuart:
"Man and Woman must be reborn into their essential
natures. That is to say, they must develop their true
essence, which is but a child. Only those with ears to hear
and eyes to see will grasp the meaning of this card. It is
telling us to awake from our sleep. At this stage we must
discard the clothing of the self; we have to stand naked,
purified."

The Tarot, Paul Foster Case: "At this stage, the adept
realizes that his personal existence is nothing but the
manifestation of the relationship between self-consciousness and subconsciousness. He sees, too, that self-consciousness and subconsciousness are not themselves personal, but are really modes of universal consciousness. At
this stage his intellectual conviction is confirmed by
fourth dimensional experiences which finally blot out the
delusion of separateness forever."

The light, the kingdom, is hidden from our conscious
realization. Mystical and transcendental experiences
remain like hidden treasures, buried from our view. Like
determined fortune hunters, we seek this buried treasure.

But the treasure is not jewel nor pearl, but wisdom and enlightenment. It must be searched for diligently and patiently if it is to offer us its riches.

The Judgment is, in the final analysis, both imminent and omnipresent. Who knows when we will be called to account for our deeds? The light shining in our inner selves will eventually illumine all that exists there.

21 The World/Sun ☉

We see the Earth as if we are looking at it from space. Until man landed on the Moon in 1969, we had never before in recorded history seen our planet in all its resplendent, glorious, and dramatic beauty.

Our Earth has a strange luminescence around it. It is the aura of the world. The aura shows that the world is alive. It is subject to birth and death as we are—it is subject to the laws of the universe as we are. It is also our parent, and we are, quite literally, "the children of the world."

The World represents wholeness, creativity, and creation. It is the symbol for latent power and the power to bring things into manifestation. The World is a balanced synergy of the elements: fire, water, earth, and air. Through balanced use of creative powers, ideas become manifested into form. Spirit becomes matter.

ASTROLOGICAL INTERPRETATION

The Sun is a large star that is the center of our solar system and a giver of life. Without the rays of the Sun, which reach us from 93 million miles away, life on Earth would not exist. Through the solar reactions on the other elements, life comes into being.

The Sun is the all-pervading creative power in nature, the masculine principle of conscious energy, the principle of fatherhood and authority. Sun worship of primitive peoples was awe and respect for this source of energy, light, heat, and growth—contrasting with the cold and darkness of the night.

The Sun, through Leo, rules the heart and the spinal column, both of which are centers in their own right, the heart for obvious reasons, and the spine as the central column of the skeletal system.

The Sun sign of Leo represents the center of our personality, and the means to self-expression. The symbol for the Sun, a circle with a dot in the middle, represents the human spirit or consciousness. The circle implies completeness and divine spirit, while the dot represents the nucleus. (The Sun itself is a giant nuclear reactor.) The Sun is the seed of potential individual manifestation of human spirit or consciousness.

The Sun primarily implies creativity. It also suggests talent in the performing arts, the theater, and the entertainment industry as a whole. Leadership and authority are also represented. There is an ability to act as a "center," leading and managing, and a talent for organizational work. The Sun implies success through a skillful handling and managing of diverse elements and energies into a cohesive and comprehensive whole.

The Sun shows a positive, happy, "sunny" outlook and augurs well for popularity and success. The negative aspects of this card imply arrogance, vanity, an overbearing attitude, delusions of grandeur, and snobbery.

TRADITIONAL INTERPRETATION

Attainment. Ultimate change. Completion. Perfection. Success. Admiration of others. Triumph in undertakings.

COMMENTARY

Tarot Classic, Stuart Kaplan: "They [describing the four cherubic figures in the Tarot Classic deck version of The World] also represent the four elements, fire, water, earth, and air, which are balanced to form the basis of life on earth and the composition of each day."

The Tarot: Path to Self Development, Micheline Stuart: "Mother Nature in all her nakedness confronts us. Her laws are stronger than we are. Two giants, pride and vanity, dominate us and we are ruled by them. Yet to become truly masters of our nature is our raison d'être [reason to be]. Imagining that we are already masters of ourselves, we ruin and violate our lives. However, if our desire to improve our condition is a genuine wish to return to our source, and is not for self aggrandizement, we will hear the trumpet blast sounded by an angel from on high."

This is a stern reminder that success is easily followed by failure, if we allow ego to be our master and are not masters of our ego. We are given creative power, but must learn to use it for the good of all, the good of the world, and not for our own selves alone.

We have the world at our feet. It is up to us whether we walk gently or trample all underfoot.

0 *The Fool/Earth* ⊕

The unnumbered Fool falls both at the beginning and end of the deck. The Fool in the One World deck has shed his material form and stands, as if naked, his arms outstretched to the universe that encompasses him.

"I am Alpha and Omega, the Beginning and the End, that which was, that which is, and that which is to come."

The Fool is spiritual essence itself—that which is formless—that substance from which all form is created.

Man, having forgotten or ignored his spiritual and divine self, is the Fool. He seeks pleasure where there is none, and stability when there is only endless change. He has forgotten who he truly is.

In truth, each being is created by the infinite, and from whence he came, he must ultimately return.

The cross symbolizes the light and the life, spirit and matter joined in endless play, a promise of eternal life and resurrection.

The Fool has shed his material body and returned to his essence.

ASTROLOGICAL INTERPRETATION

The Fool, at both the beginning and the end of the sequence, reminds us of the divinity and infinity of all life. The physical form we have acquired is temporary, and we must strive for the spiritual. Man is the Fool when he forgets his divine origins.

The Fool, bridging both the beginning and the end, denotes that we must be alert for overzealous spirituality and disregard for practical matters. It may also represent someone who is too materialistic in his or her approach to life, and who ignores spirituality.

TRADITIONAL INTERPRETATION

Folly. Immaturity. Levity. Irrationality. Lack of discipline. Indiscretion. Inattentiveness to detail.

COMMENTARY

Tarot Classic, Stuart Kaplan: "The Fool is entering upon a new world of unlimited possibilities and self-expression."

This journey can be seen to be the ultimate journey, that from spirit (En Soph) to matter (Malkuth) and back again.

Jung and the Tarot, Sally Nichols: "In the Marseilles Tarot, The Fool is numbered zero, a fact worthy of our attention, for the number under which a card was 'born' sheds light on its character and destiny. Like the stars, numbers shine with an eternal reality that transcends language and geography." She continues, "The Fool has been linked to the Kaballistic En Soph or Limitless Light, the active principle of existence prior to its manifestation in matter, the nothing from which all things proceed. As such it is also the alchemical *prima materia*, or ground of being, the stuff we all start with. The circle also symbolizes the Garden of Eden, that blissful state of unconsciousness and innocence that mankind experienced before consciousness. Both psychologically and physically we create the world we see. Everything in it comes from nothing at our birth and we will return to nothing at our death. This nothing is outside time and space. It is pure nature, the essence behind the veil."

By describing the Fool thus, we can see that he knows he is divine and immortal. He was there before all things came into being, and will be there when they return.

The Fool is the jester, the child within, which is innocent and holy. He is pure spirit.

The Fool is there at the beginning, as he is at the end. He is eternal and immortal. The Fool allows himself to be foolish because he laughs in innocence.

Once the Fool has again manifested into matter, and reenters the cycle of incarnation, he becomes The Magician.

THE MINOR ARCANA

FIRE

Ace of Batons

The Ace of Batons represents the element of fire and expresses the powers attributable to all the fire signs: Aries, Leo, and Sagittarius.

Fire signs are creative, independent, bold, forceful, domineering, extroverted, pioneering, fearless, far-sighted, warm, friendly, gregarious, and creative—shining with an inner light.

The Ace, or number one, represents the primal power of fire and all its qualities, the beginning of all creative endeavors and enterprises. It provides the power to initialize, conceptualize, and organize.

TRADITIONAL INTERPRETATION

Creativity, fertility. The primal energy and vigor of the element of fire. The beginning of something new, the launching of fresh enterprises, the foundation of future success.

REVERSED

Delays and setbacks in both creative and business projects. Bad planning and management. Lack of foresight, hastiness, and impatience. Badly conceived plans. Not a good sign for the beginning of any project—plans should be thoroughly reviewed, delayed, or postponed when this card is drawn in reverse.

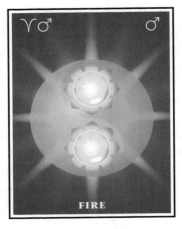

Two of Batons

FIRST SUBDIVISION OF ARIES

NATURAL RULER: MARS

SUBRULER: MARS

A ries is the bold, fearless initiator of the zodiac. Here in the first subdivision, also ruled by Mars, the energy is doubly forceful, determined, bold, pioneering. There is a need and determination to succeed, and great leadership ability coupled with the power to initiate projects.

TRADITIONAL INTERPRETATION

Great strength and determination of will. Firm rulership. Courage and initiative. Earned success.

REVERSED

Overly ambitious. Pride, ego, danger of arrogant and ill-conceived plans. Overly forceful. Failure due to over-aggression, lack of planning, impatience. Bad relations with others due to domineering and dictatorial manner and insensitivity. Always wanting to be "number one." Indecisive, confused, muddled, lacking proper direction.

Three of Batons

SECOND SUBDIVISION OF ARIES

NATURAL RULER: MARS

SUBRULER: SUN

The strength of Aries is here given the bonus of the powerful and noble creative energy of the Sun, who rules this subdivision. Therefore, there will be strong qualities of organization, visualization, leadership, and excellence in creative projects and ventures.

TRADITIONAL INTERPRETATION

The successful launching of creative projects. Original ideas and inspiration. Strength supported by high motives and ideals. The card of the artist or inventor who turns dreams into reality.

REVERSED

Arrogance, pride. Overly ambitious, dictatorial attitudes. Delays and setbacks, badly conceived plans, bad leadership, egotistical attitudes, and tyranny.

Four of Batons

THIRD SUBDIVISION OF ARIES

NATURAL RULER: MARS

SUBRULER: VENUS

The boldness, independence and assertiveness of Aries in the third subdivision is muted by the gentle and thoughtful influence of Venus as subruler. This gives the Four of Batons artistic qualities and a much more loving, gentle disposition and manner. The energy is still determined. Strong passions, love of pleasure, and love of the arts are brought by Venus, who also makes the influence of Aries kindlier and more directed to harmony and cooperation.

TRADITIONAL INTERPRETATION

Success in the realm of ideas. The card of the successful and skilled designer. Order, establishment of beauty and elegance, civilization, refinement and culture. Romance. Society. Harmony. Prosperity. Peace. Tranquility.

REVERSED

Failure of projects, possibly through excesses, self-indulgence and decadence. Uncouth, unrefined, uncivilized. Waste of creative talent. Perverse, indecisive, lazy. Lack of harmony. Argumentative and contrary nature.

Five of Batons

FIRST SUBDIVISION OF LEO

NATURAL RULER: SUN

SUBRULER: SATURN

Leo is a powerful and creative sign, usually with a "sunny" disposition. However, with Saturn subruling, there is a tendency toward poverty and trouble, and a lack of sympathy in the nature, which is austere and proud. A natural caution and lack of self-confidence manifests when Saturn casts his shadow, and either there will be much restriction and delays in creative endeavors and personal affairs, or one will have to work unusually hard to achieve one's aims, given the difficult and constrictive influences of this energy. The Five of Batons also indicates a need for more structure and discipline in creative projects and endeavors and may indicate failure due to lack of foresight and planning.

TRADITIONAL INTERPRETATION

Conflict and opposition. Delays and setbacks that require great efforts to be overcome. Tests to be dealt with before progress can resume. Unsatisfied desires. Struggle. Strife. Conflict.

REVERSED

Obstacles. Fraud, defeat. Trickery. Complexity. Delays and setbacks. Unhelpful influences. Miserly, dictatorial, materialistic. Lack of planning or stable foundations. Harsh, dictatorial, lacking in feeling.

Six of Batons

SECOND SUBDIVISION OF LEO

NATURAL RULER: THE SUN

SUBRULER: JUPITER

The beneficent influence of the Sun is given great good fortune by the subrulership of the benevolent Jupiter. Usually fortunate in creative ventures and romantic matters with a kind, noble, and humane disposition, this is a very fortunate and favorable combination. The Six of Batons means success in love and the performing arts, luck in gambling and investments, and in all creative projects. It also indicates a generous and expansive nature. Endeavors could be connected with foreign countries.

TRADITIONAL INTERPRETATION

Conquest. Triumph. The arrival of great news. Successful speculation. Gain. Advancement. The realization of efforts and desires. Victory and the fulfillment of all projects. Success through originality and hard work. Satisfaction. Skill. Diplomacy.

REVERSED

Delays, setbacks. Unlucky. Unfortunate. Loss of opportunity. Overly expansive, over-confident. Lack in direction and lack of effort may result in failure. Over-optimistic, lacking foresight and constructive planning.

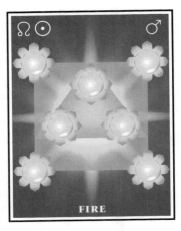

FIRE

Seven of Batons

THIRD SUBDIVISION OF LEO

NATURAL RULER: THE SUN

SUBRULER: MARS

Leo with subruler of Mars indicates a strong, forcible nature, desiring to rule. The power of leadership and organizational skills are mixed with creativity and daring. The Seven of Batons can signify an adventurous person, bold and commanding, generous in success and in defeat. This person enjoys challenges and is usually victorious and successful in creative projects. The emphasis is on the courage to overcome adversaries and to succeed by surmounting obstacles and overwhelming odds.

TRADITIONAL INTERPRETATION

A time of great possibility. Success is within reach. Victory. Gain. Competition overcome through consistent and daring efforts. Triumph through personal courage and creative abilities.

REVERSED

Failure through aggressive and arrogant attitudes. Misuse of power. Loss of opportunity, possibly squandered. Defeat in the face of great challenges. Hesitation, indecision, lack of motivation, lack of ideals.

Eight of Batons

FIRST SUBDIVISION OF SAGITTARIUS

NATURAL RULER: JUPITER

SUBRULER: MERCURY

The fortunate and creative sign of Sagittarius is here given the quick intellect of Mercury as subruler to add to its abilities. There will be much communication and travel, a quick intellect with great versatility and good judgment. Inspiration is expressed through the spoken or written word with an emphasis on the expansive and spiritual qualities of Sagittarius. News, especially from abroad, is to be expected, and all communications should be fortunate with this influence. Study is particularly emphasized with a potential for success.

TRADITIONAL INTERPRETATION

Sudden progress or movement. Hopeful change. The ending of delays. A good time for taking the initiative or grasping suitable opportunities. Favorable for news and communications. Important journeys may be indicated, especially overseas.

REVERSED

Delays and setbacks in news, communications, or travel. Confusion. Indecision. Impatience. A tendency to be overly optimistic or to scatter energy without an appropriate outlet. Loss of opportunity. Disputes, quarrels, and discord. Lack of, or over emphasis on, detail.

Nine of Batons

SECOND SUBDIVISION OF SAGITTARIUS

NATURAL RULER: JUPITER

SUBRULER: THE MOON

Love of romance, home, and family and a strong imagination accompany the influence of the Moon as subruler of the second subdivision of Sagittarius. The native may live abroad, and there is a great love of travel. Inheritance or legacy and a chance of great success are indicated with these influences. The influence of the Nine of Batons alternates between expansive and contractive and is often restless and changeable. Profound sensitivity and foresight accompanies a sympathetic and generous nature.

TRADITIONAL INTERPRETATION

Strength and stability. Courage.

REVERSED

Hidden enemies. Lack of insight. Imbalance between contraction and expansion. Lack of compassion. Lack of vision. Delays in travel or moving home. Loss of patronage or inheritance. Changeable, restless, unreliable, clinging, and noncommittal. Moody.

Ten of Batons

THIRD SUBDIVISION OF SAGITTARIUS

NATURAL RULER: JUPITER

SUBRULER: SATURN

The naturally expansive and jovial nature of Sagittarius is made more cautious, serious, and sober by the influence of Saturn. The passions will be strong, but controlled. There will be a love of structured study and in-depth research into the philosophical and scientific—demanding patience and dedication. An unusual ability to sustain effort means that although the usual Saturnian obstacles may appear on the querent's path, in true optimistic Sagittarian style, they will eventually be overcome, and success achieved.

TRADITIONAL INTERPRETATION

Triumph and great good fortune after a period of setbacks and delays.

REVERSED

Delays, setbacks. Oppressive responsibilities. Lack of freedom. Pessimism. Lack of opportunity. Deceit. Lack of funds, or lack of structure to a project.

EARTH

Ace of Coins

The Ace of Coins represents the element of earth and expresses the powers attributable to all the earth signs: Taurus, Virgo, and Capricorn.

Earth signs are usually earthy, practical, plodding, precise, fastidious, self-repressive and introverted, with an aptitude for form and foundation, and an affinity with nature. They are capable of slow and steady effort, careful planning, and calculation, and are reliable and trustworthy, being solid and dependable.

The Ace represents the absolute power of the earth element and all its qualities. It signifies the beginning of financial and business matters, abundance in material wealth, property, and tangible material assets.

TRADITIONAL INTERPRETATION

Prosperity. Great wealth. Firm foundations, possessions, security, and appreciation of physical form, sensuousness. Sensation. The stability of the element earth. Steadfast. Dependable.

REVERSED

Loss. Possible financial ruin. Excessive materialism. Greed. Misuse of material wealth and possessions. Dependent on the senses. Lack of insight and spirituality.

EARTH

Two of Coins

FIRST SUBDIVISION OF TAURUS

NATURAL RULER: VENUS

SUBRULER: MERCURY

The slow, sensuous, and practical sign of Taurus is here endowed with the swift energy of Mercury as ruler of the first subdivision. Mercury bestows a highly endowed and practical mind, poetic and artistic, with a keen sense of detailed design. The Two of Coins shows a nature that is fond of the artistic and beautiful, sensuous, and desirous of ease, comfort, and luxury. Business sense is enhanced. A communicative and artistic nature indicates success in drama, music, and art. The Two of Coins shows fruitfulness in the realm of ideas.

TRADITIONAL INTERPRETATION

Literary ability. Agility in handling money matters. Change in material circumstances. Movement, change, and news or communications are imminent. Travel connected with business. Progress. Success. Skill. Development. Rewards.

REVERSED

Delays and setbacks in money or property matters. Delays or misunderstandings in communications relating to property or material possessions. Overly critical and stubborn. Lack of ideas.

EARTH

Three of Coins

SECOND SUBDIVISION OF TAURUS

NATURAL RULER: VENUS

SUBRULER: MOON

The changeability and emotionality of the Moon, added to the stability and sensuality of Taurus, give a romantic and imaginative disposition, love of pleasure, love of home and family. The Three of Coins signifies someone sensuous, sensitive and artistic, with a love of food and luxurious possessions. Success is in property matters related to the home and business, especially connected to food and restaurants. An ability to conserve and construct is present. The Three of Coins can indicate someone who is sometimes stubborn or clinging.

TRADITIONAL INTERPRETATION

Skill in trade or work. Artistic ability. Successful progress in business. Original and consistent. Rewards and success to projects begun at this time. Comfort.

REVERSED

Obstinacy. Fixed ideas. Lack of skill. Overly cautious in business matters, lack of insight, confusion. Refusal to review situations. Clinging to outdated ideas. Lack of financial support, especially relating to the home. Emotional considerations relating to material things.

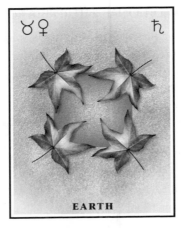

EARTH

Four of Coins

THIRD SUBDIVISION OF TAURUS

NATURAL RULER: VENUS

SUBRULER: SATURN

The restrictive influence of Saturn in the third subdivision of Taurus indicates delays and setbacks in material concerns. It can indicate poverty or extreme difficulty achieving material stability, miserliness, and a lack of opportunity. On the positive side, there is a prospect of material success and stability due to consistent effort and sensible structure and planning. Should the positive aspect of Saturn apply, success will be late—but lasting—provided that the querent tackles obstacles slowly and sensibly.

TRADITIONAL INTERPRETATION

Love of material wealth. Hoarder. Skinflint. Miser. Inability to share. Setbacks. Obstacles. Opposition. Complete material stability after a delay. The establishment of a financial empire on firm foundations. Monetary problems overcome.

REVERSED

Setbacks. Delays. Ruin. Loss. Lack of financial support. Oppression. Material want. Excessively materialistic. Miserly. Inability to delegate. Bureaucratic and oppressive. Fear of poverty.

EARTH

Five of Coins

FIRST SUBDIVISION OF VIRGO

NATURAL RULER: MERCURY

SUBRULER: SUN

At first glance, the influence of the Sun is positive in this subdivision. Indeed, it adds qualities of creativity, confidence, and leadership to the normally unassuming Virgo. However, the unstable influence of the number five, and the combustive influence of the Sun and Mercury in such close contact mean that the communicative and normally logical thought processes of the analytical and critical Virgo, ruled by the swift thinking Mercury, are now channeled almost entirely through the ego (through the Sun's rulership of the dramatic sign of Leo), distorting objective thinking. Financial loss can occur through weak judgment, poor planning, and overconfidence. The positive qualities of this combination can be expressed successfully when the nature of this energy is comprehended.

TRADITIONAL INTERPRETATION

Material problems. Loss. Failure. Error.

REVERSED

Imminent loss. Confusion. Over-speculation.

EARTH

Six of Coins

SECOND SUBDIVISION OF VIRGO

NATURAL RULER: MERCURY

SUBRULER: VENUS

The keen intellect of Mercury operating through Virgo is complemented by the artistic and literary talent of Venus. The Six of Coins indicates a gentle and kind nature and a pleasing disposition, success in business and property matters. The arts are well starred, with a keenly critical appreciation of form and design, and a love of harmony.

TRADITIONAL INTERPRETATION

Balance and solvency in financial matters. Generosity. Philanthropy. Charity. Kindness. Material gain.

REVERSED

Avarice. Selfishness. Debts. Poor investments. Over or underemphasis on detail. Indecision, poor judgment, imbalance, unsound advice.

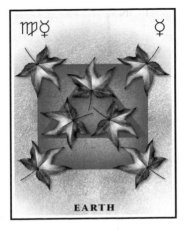

EARTH

Seven of Coins

THIRD SUBDIVISION OF VIRGO

NATURAL RULER: MERCURY

SUBRULER: MERCURY

Versatility characterizes this subdivision ruled by Mercury, which is also the natural ruler of Virgo. The Seven of Coins has a scientific bent and an aptitude for literature and the arts, as well as a keen business sense. Medicine, teaching, diet, and hygiene are also areas of interest. This subdivision further indicates a particularly keen intellect, a perfectionist, who can tend to overanalyze, and whose nature can be cold and critical.

TRADITIONAL INTERPRETATION

Ingenuity. Growth. Hard work. Progress. Successful deal-ings. Money. Wealth. Possible material success if inertia can be overcome. Swift action is needed.

REVERSED

Logic without imagination. Fruitless tasks. One's efforts may be in vain. Loss. Disappointment. Ideas that are impractical. Fatigue.

EARTH

Eight of Coins

FIRST SUBDIVISION OF CAPRICORN

NATURAL RULER: SATURN

SUBRULER: JUPITER

Jupiter adds an expansive tone to the first subdivision, and indicates ambition and the necessary drive and good fortune to achieve lofty goals. Positive changes and the speeding up of all matters are to be expected. There may be travel connected with business or foreign contacts. This card often indicates high positions and political ambitions.

TRADITIONAL INTERPRETATION

Fortunate change in material circumstances. Effort bringing rewards. Success for those with energy or talent. Quick to learn. Hard work. Personal effort.

REVERSED

Unfortunate. Unlucky. Misjudged business opportunities. Lack of support. Fearful. Miserly. Poor planning.

Nine of Coins

SECOND SUBDIVISION OF CAPRICORN

NATURAL RULER: SATURN

SUBRULER: MARS

Mars adds enthusiasm and ambition to the second subdivision of Capricorn, as well as leadership skills and an optimistic slant. Energy and determination characterize this combination, and the natives can reach high office, especially in the areas ruled by Mars. One may have a tendency to domineering and social climbing with a view to social, material, and political conquest.

TRADITIONAL INTERPRETATION

Material success. Comfort. Popularity. Accomplishment. Sound administrator.

REVERSED

Collapse. Ruin. Fall from grace. Arguments. Quarrels. Competition. Arrogant. Out of touch. Failure.

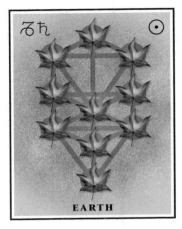

Ten of Coins

THIRD SUBDIVISION OF CAPRICORN

NATURAL RULER: SATURN

SUBRULER: SUN

The Sun adds organizational and creative ability to the third subdivision of Capricorn, and can produce prosperity and wealth for the person drawing this card, due to the steady development of creative skills and talents. Ten of Coins signifies endurance and success. The children of the querent may also be talented and profit from this influence.

TRADITIONAL INTERPRETATION

Prosperity. Security. Family. Ancestry. Inheritance. Blood ties. Family wealth. Material security.

REVERSED

Loss of status. Downfall. Poor risk. Loss of inheritance. Delays.

AIR

Ace of Swords

The Ace of Swords represents the element of air and expresses the powers attributable to all the air signs: Gemini, Libra, and Aquarius.

Air signs are often mentally or intellectually oriented, logical, detached, and rational. The impartiality and unemotional tendencies of the air signs make them objective and fair, giving a direct association with judgments, order, and authority. Their detachment can often make them seem cold or aloof and out of touch with their own feelings. They are strategists, writers, and inventors—full of ideas and innovations. All the air signs work on duality. Gemini is the twins, Libra, the scales, and Aquarius the two currents of electricity—AC/DC. Air signs are hard to pin down, changeable and erratic. They dislike restrictions to their intellectual freedom.

The Ace represents the totality of the combined power of all the air signs and signifies the beginning of all new projects that require mental agility and inventive genius. This may include literary projects, artistic ventures and inventions, or any new ideas, plans, or projects in general.

TRADITIONAL INTERPRETATION

Great determination. Force. Activity. Power. Success. Fertility. Prosperity. Victory. Justice and authority. The faculty of thought. Success of all enterprises. Progress. Changes.

REVERSED

Restriction. Injustice. Tyranny. Obstacles. Hindrance. Failure of plans and projects. Negative outcome. Bad ideas, badly formulated plans. Miscalculation. Slander.

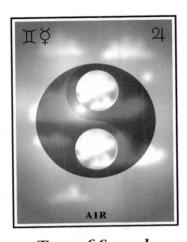

Two of Swords

FIRST SUBDIVISION OF GEMINI

NATURAL RULER: MERCURY

SUBRULER: JUPITER

Jupiter adds a thoughtful and expansive tone to the Mercurial Gemini. It gives a kind and generous disposition and adds self-confidence. The normally dualistic Gemini is given philosophical insight and a keen intellect here, with a propensity to judicial and legal pursuits, as well as talent with the written and spoken word. However, a profusion of ideas requires sound judgment through which to filter the numerous impressions that pour in, and a misuse of faculties should be avoided at all costs.

TRADITIONAL INTERPRETATION

Equilibrium. Truth. Peace and justice. Balanced force. The relationship between opposing forces.

REVERSED

Arguments. Quarrels. Discord. Opposing factions. Ideas working against each other. Bad mediation. Lack of improvement. Tension. Trickery. Deceit.

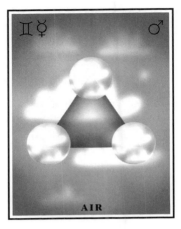

Three of Swords

SECOND SUBDIVISION OF GEMINI

NATURAL RULER: MERCURY

SUBRULER: MARS

Mars adds much aggression and force to the nervous and skittish Gemini, thus making for a quarrelsome and aggressive personality. Love of debate and a powerful need to excel in all areas is governed by this sign. The Three of Swords can indicate a loud and pushy personality, with a taste for verbal conflict and argument. Put to positive use, this energy makes for ambition and dedication in all areas governed by Gemini, especially journalists, salespeople, singers, and writers.

TRADITIONAL INTERPRETATION

Strife and conflict. Destruction.

REVERSED

War. Disorder. Danger, especially during short distance journeys. Violence. Arguments. Oppression. Bullying. Impatience. Unreliability.

Four of Swords

THIRD SUBDIVISION OF GEMINI

NATURAL RULER: MERCURY

SUBRULER: SUN

The creative powers of the Sun are added in abundance to the literary and talented Gemini in this subdivision. A love of drama, theater, and literature gives success in intellectual matters. The nature may be somewhat haughty and changeable but eventual success in the areas ruled by Gemini is greatly enhanced by the presence of the Sun.

TRADITIONAL INTERPRETATION

Peace and order. Rest. Recuperation. Relaxation. Entertainment.

REVERSED

Depression. Lack of confidence. Nervousness. Inflated ideas. Grandiose plans. Failure in creative and literary projects or, at least, a need for a thorough review. Overly critical. Imminent collapse of plans. Failure.

Five of Swords

FIRST SUBDIVISION OF LIBRA

NATURAL RULER: VENUS

SUBRULER: MOON

The rapidly changing face of the Moon gives a restless and weak nature, easily influenced emotionally in this first subdivision of Libra. There may be extravagance and unreliable habits, with a characteristic indecisiveness. Women (or the mother), home, and family are especially affected. There can be an aptitude in general business and gains in the public sector and property matters.

TRADITIONAL INTERPRETATION

Defeat, loss, and dishonor. Instability. Humiliation.
Conflict. Hidden motives. Difficulties. Power complex.
Hidden capabilities.

REVERSED

Imminent loss. Failure.

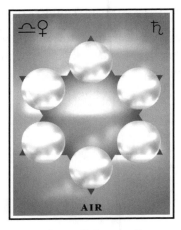

Six of Swords

SECOND SUBDIVISION OF LIBRA

NATURAL RULER: VENUS

SUBRULER: SATURN

Saturn brings grief and trouble to this subdivision but promises success after obstacles and difficulties have been overcome, or toward the latter half of the life. Difficulties may be many and may relate to marriage or partnerships in general, but there is a steadfastness with this subdivision that enables problems to be resolved eventually in both personal and business matters.

TRADITIONAL INTERPRETATION

The solving of problems. Removal of obstacles. Progress resumed. End of sorrow and worry. Moving away from imminent danger. Travel or a new home. Harmonious circumstances and surroundings. Success after anxiety.

REVERSED

Obstacles. Delays. Restrictions. Domineering. Conceited. Selfish.

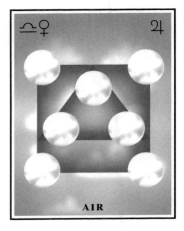

Seven of Swords

THIRD SUBDIVISION OF LIBRA

NATURAL RULER: VENUS

SUBRULER: JUPITER

The harmonious nature of Libra coupled with the expansive and beneficent Jupiter promises a happy and successful outcome to ventures, a generous, well-balanced, and creative mind, a happy and successful marriage, and many long-distance journeys overseas. Legal matters are well-starred, suggesting triumph over adversaries.

TRADITIONAL INTERPRETATION

Hope. Confidence. Intelligence. Powerful opposition. Confrontation that requires subtle ingenuity. Courage and perseverance.

REVERSED

Limited success. Over-confidence. Loss. Dishonor. Wasted opportunity.

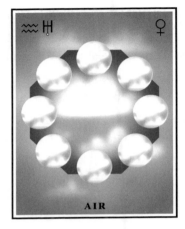

AIR

Eight of Swords

FIRST SUBDIVISION OF AQUARIUS

NATURAL RULER: URANUS

SUBRULER: VENUS

The humane nature of Aquarius is blessed with the presence of Venus in the first subdivision. A high degree of intelligence and success in science and the fine arts is present, with gain through inventive or ingenious ideas, literature, and musical talent. The Eight of Swords is friendly and humane, and success is promised in the areas governed by both ruler and subruler of this subdivision. This card may also indicate the unpredictable.

TRADITIONAL INTERPRETATION

Highly intelligent, inquiring mind. Resourceful. Indicates intellectual study. Patient effort and attention to detail. The end of adversity. Changes for the better. Opportunities must be grasped.

REVERSED

Domineering. Impersonal. Unexpected changes. Progress halted. Ideas that are too eccentric or implausible to succeed. Perverse and cruel. Self-indulgent. Spiteful, especially in love. Isolation.

Nine of Swords

SECOND SUBDIVISION OF AQUARIUS

NATURAL RULER: URANUS

SUBRULER: MERCURY

The inventive genius of Aquarius is given intellectual capabilities by the presence of Mercury. The mind is both scientific and philosophical with an aptitude for inventive ideas especially in medicine and hygiene. Math, astronomy and occult research are indicated. An independent spirit and a penetrating mind are characteristic of this subdivision. An impersonal streak to this combination can make a lack of emotion and cruelty of speech evident.

TRADITIONAL INTERPRETATION

Success and gain after persistent effort. Cruelty, unreasonable passions, anxiety. Misery. Quarrel. Strength and new life arising from suffering. The card of the martyr.

REVERSED

Tyranny. Cruelty. Failure through eccentric and confused thinking. Clever but devious. Impractical Ideas. Scandal. Gossip. Malice.

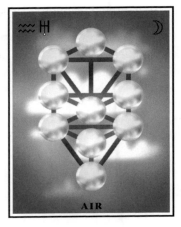

AIR

Ten of Swords

THIRD SUBDIVISION OF AQUARIUS

NATURAL RULER: URANUS

SUBRULER: THE MOON

The Moon ruling this subdivision indicates change-ability and melancholy, solitude, strange terrors and weird experiences. An instability in the emotional nature may be cruel and impersonal, and the tendency is to unusual or erratic behavior. Family matters may be unpredictable or unreliable.

TRADITIONAL INTERPRETATION

Ruin, pain, affliction. Sadness. Mental Anguish. Desolation. Grief. Problems with groups and societies. However, there is cause for hope, as the cycle of misfortune may be at an end, and things may take a turn for the better.

REVERSED

Imminent danger. False hopes and wishes. Discord. Continuation of suffering. No end in sight. Confusion. Oppression.

WATER

Ace of Cups

The Ace of Cups represents the passive, feminine element of water and expresses the powers attributable to all the water signs: Cancer, Scorpio, and Pisces.

Water signs are usually introverted, repressive, extremely intuitive and psychically sensitive, emotional, caring and compassionate. They "feel" their way through situations and are not usually intellectually inclined, preferring to use their intuition as opposed to logic.

The Ace represents the absolute power of the water element and all its qualities, and signifies new beginnings in the sphere of the emotions and emotional relationships—love, home, family, and motherhood.

TRADITIONAL INTERPRETATION

Great abundance. Fulfillment. Fertility. Fullness. Happiness. Productiveness. Goodness. Marriage. The birth of a child. Artistic or psychic abilities. Nourishment. Protection. The process of creation. Fruitfulness. Love. Motherhood.

REVERSED

Barrenness. Failure. Stagnation. Despair. Lack of love and sympathy. Loneliness. Depression. Disappointments in love. Change. Instability. Unrequited love. End of, or serious difficulties in, love or family relationships. Unloving. Lacking vision. Ignoring feelings or intuition. Misuse of, or dangerous emotions.

Two of Cups

FIRST SUBDIVISION OF CANCER

NATURAL RULER: MOON

SUBRULER: VENUS

Cancer benefits from Venus in this first subdivision, as Venus adds luxury, sensuality, sociability, and generosity to the normally domestic and introverted Crab. It brings success in social and artistic matters, possibly through partnership, and a fondness for entertainment and pleasure.

TRADITIONAL INTERPRETATION

Love. Emotional affinity. Understanding. Friendship. Marriage. Engagement. Forgiveness and tolerance. Passion. Union. Understanding. Cooperation. End of disagreements or arguments.

REVERSED

Problems in relationships. Conflict. Quarrels. Divorce. End of engagement. Separation. Discord. Deceit. Emotional self-indulgence. Underhandedness. Gossip. Emotional excess. Unsatisfactory love or false friends. Misunderstanding.

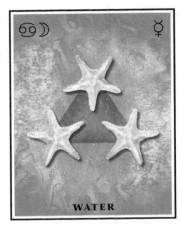

WATER

Three of Cups

SECOND SUBDIVISION OF CANCER

NATURAL RULER: MOON

SUBRULER: MERCURY

The intuitive and homey nature of Cancer is given strong intellectual and creative capabilities with the presence of Mercury in the second subdivision. There is literary ability, a strong imagination, and a love of travel. The home may be a place of study, or a place of much coming and going. Diet and hygiene may also be important.

TRADITIONAL INTERPRETATION

Security. A comfortable home. Good family life. Happiness and good fortune. Spiritual or psychic growth or study. News regarding a marriage or birth. Maternity, abundant fertility. Resolution of problems. Healing. Solace. Satisfactory results. Fulfillment. Compromise.

REVERSED

Confusion. Delays. Domestic problems. Lack of stability. Emotional coldness. Exploitation. Loss. Unhappiness.

Four of Cups

THIRD SUBDIVISION OF CANCER

NATURAL RULER: MOON

SUBRULER: MOON

The Four of Cups represents a highly sensitive and intuitive individual, and indicates a compassionate nature, love of home, family, and romance. Public recognition and success in property matters, often through the patronage of women, or the mother, may indicate a change of residence. The double influence of the Moon indicates rapidly shifting moods and emotions and an overly sensitive nature.

TRADITIONAL INTERPRETATION

Fondness for the home or mother. Inner mystical experience. Material success. Gain through marriage or inheritance. Travel. Change in residence. Too much of a good thing. Happiness that has reached a peak and can proceed no further.

REVERSED

Boredom. Stagnation. Dissatisfaction. Overly emotional, fearful. Unstable. Over-indulgence. Unhappiness. Emotional turmoil. Bitterness.

Five of Cups

FIRST SUBDIVISION OF SCORPIO

NATURAL RULER: MARS/PLUTO

SUBRULER: MARS

The first subdivision of Scorpio, ruled by Mars, gives a strong, forceful and energetic influence. However, the combative nature of this subdivision makes for difficulties in relationships, with power struggles or a need for control and revenge, or both. The ambitions are strong and willful in business, but personal life may be dominated by excessive and strange love affairs.

TRADITIONAL INTERPRETATION

Harmony replaced by worry and loss. Regret. Destruction. Disregard for the feelings of others. Melancholy. Disappointment.

REVERSED

Cruelty. Vengeance. Aggression. Domination. Loss. Strife. Quarrel.

Six of Cups

SECOND SUBDIVISION OF SCORPIO

NATURAL RULER: MARS/PLUTO

SUBRULER: THE SUN

The Sun ruling this second subdivision of Scorpio promises creative success, honor, and fame to those who come under its influence. The stamina and dedication of Scorpio energy is given an abundance of creativity and masterful governing qualities by the Sun. Those under its influence may be proud or even tyrannical in their methods.

TRADITIONAL INTERPRETATION

Generosity. Self-confidence. Deep emotions. Financial gain. Pleasure. Inheritance. Happiness. Success. The realization of a dream. Elements from the past working through the present to create a new future, especially with regard to relationships, friends, or lovers.

REVERSED

Nostalgia. Domineering. Possessive. Demanding. Loss of legacy. Failure through rigidity.

WATER

Seven of Cups

THIRD SUBDIVISION OF SCORPIO

NATURAL RULER: MARS/PLUTO

SUBRULER: VENUS

Venus adds grace and charm, artistic ability, and sociability to the third subdivision of the intense, secretive and mystical sign of Scorpio. There may be a strong amorous nature and a deep interest in mysticism and mystical art. However, the already strong sexual nature of Scorpio is made further prone to excess in love affairs, with strong passions that are quick and volatile. The Seven of Cups shows a magnetic quality, and can be passionate, fickle, and steadfast at the same time. This is an intense and heady combination. Money may come from inheritances.

TRADITIONAL INTERPRETATION

Fondness for pleasure and comfort. Fantasy. Unrealistic. Imagination. Daydreams. Foolish whims. Wishful thinking. Mystical experience. A card of choice. Alternatives that must be explored, though only one is of exceptional promise. Special powers and abilities arise from the unconscious and must be tempered by reason.

REVERSED

Deception in love and friendship. Disharmony in marriage. Fantasy. Reliance on false hopes. Inaction. Cruelty. Passions. Determination. Willpower.

Eight of Cups

FIRST SUBDIVISION OF PISCES

NATURAL RULER: JUPITER AND NEPTUNE

SUBRULER: SATURN

The imaginative and sensitive sign of Pisces is given extra weight and responsibility by Saturn in the first subdivision. There may be limitations and delays, secret enemies, morbid fantasies, difficulties through love affairs, quarrels, and disputes. Depression may occur more easily than normal, and the querent may find trouble balancing high ideals with daily needs. However, if the inspirational qualities of Pisces can be harnessed and disciplined constructively by Saturn, then poetry, art, music, and drama—or dedication to a worthwhile cause or institution—can be expressed extremely successfully.

TRADITIONAL INTERPRETATION

Changes in affections and feelings. Sacrifice. Moving on. Progress. Disappointment. Shyness. Charity. Sympathy. Severing of past relationships or links with the past in order to create new growth for the future.

REVERSED

Depression. Loss. Isolation. Unrealistic. Lack of ambition. Fear of poverty. Failure. Lack of discipline. Bad moves or changes. Meanness.

Nine of Cups

SECOND SUBDIVISION OF PISCES

NATURAL RULER: JUPITER AND NEPTUNE

SUBRULER: JUPITER

Jupiter rules in this second subdivision of Pisces, indicating an expansive and mystical personality that is extremely creative (especially in the arts), and religious, philosophical, or mystical by nature. Success and high positions may be the result of the positive application of this energy. There is a beneficent and genial nature, good fortune more often than not, and a chance to rise in life. Although the nature is kind and sympathetic, a lack of constancy in relationships may arise from a great need for personal freedom.

TRADITIONAL INTERPRETATION

Emotional stability. Contentment. Kindness. Security. Good will. Affectionate. Fulfilled desires. Fondness for luxury. Creative imagination.

REVERSED

Self-delusion. Weakness. Fantasy. Lack of commitment. Conceited. Illusion. Delusions. Escapism. Lack of substance. Self-pity. Addiction.

WATER

Ten of Cups

THIRD SUBDIVISION OF PISCES

NATURAL RULER: JUPITER AND NEPTUNE

SUBRULER: MARS

The brute force of Mars merges with the inspirational and nebulous Pisces in the third subdivision. If this energy is applied and used positively, a dedicated and brave visionary or healer may be the result. There may also be artistic and musical talent. The combative tendencies of Mars can cause danger by hidden or secret enemies, possible danger during travels in foreign lands, and trouble in close partnerships and relationships. The Ten of Cups may be generally unreliable. Assistance may come from friends in high positions.

TRADITIONAL INTERPRETATION

Help and financial gain through friends or associates. Sensitive. Emotional. Peaceful and secure environment. Search for fulfillment crowned with success.

REVERSED

Disruption. Anti-social. Over-indulgence. Decadence. Self-pity. Loss. Failure.

THE COURT CARDS

BATONS: FIRE
(Aries, Leo, and Sagittarius)

FIRE

King of Batons

The fire sign male, the King of Batons, is usually confident, extroverted, and sociable. He likes to dominate in social situations and demands a lot of personal attention and admiration. He is a bright spirit with much enthusiasm, optimism, and joy. He is warm, affectionate and passionate. He has the power to initiate and manage large-scale projects and is fearless and ardent both at work and at play. The King of Batons enjoys personal challenge and is an adventurer, explorer, and initiator.

REVERSED

Arrogant and headstrong, the reversed King of Batons is a bullying, critical, and intolerant person. He believes himself to be in the right and more deserving than others. He is selfish and self-centered, domineering, and aggressive. He has no direction and no goals.

FIRE

Queen of Batons

The fire sign female, the Queen of Batons, is a generous and commanding woman. Extroverted and in control of herself, the fire sign female is confident and self-assured, sociable and outgoing. She can be magnetic, proud and determined, and very independent.

Like her male counterpart, she is also warm, enthusiastic, and well-suited to positions of authority or organization. She is friendly and charming. Although she is a very practical and efficient person, she is often psychic and very spiritual, in her own way.

REVERSED

An interfering, bossy woman, insensitive to others' needs and determined to have her own way, the reversed Queen of Batons is aggressive and indifferent to all but herself. Dominating and loudly spoken, taking advice from no one and depending on everyone, the reversed Queen is ambitious, neurotic, egotistical, and grasping.

FIRE

Prince of Batons

The young Prince of Batons is an affectionate and sociable youth, adventurous, bold, and determined. He is creative in many ways and easy to teach. He is enthusiastic and keen to learn. He is naive, very gullible, and needs firm but kind discipline to keep him from straying. He is a good student and has many contributions of his own to make later in life. He should be encouraged, as the Prince of Batons is sensitive underneath his confident exterior and any hurts or rejections will not be forgotten. Encourage him to do his best, and he will.

REVERSED

The reversed Prince of Batons is a loud, rebellious youth, brazen and bold. He will disrupt proceedings merely to gain attention, of which he needs a lot, and will not be satisfied until he has it. He may be spoilt or demanding, but the Prince of Batons will insist on equality and his fair share. He will also howl very loudly until he gets it. The Prince of Batons needs a firm, but gentle hand to show him the error of his ways. The reversed Prince also needs much affection.

FIRE

Princess of Batons

The young Princess of Batons, the yet-to-be Queen, is full of life and love. Innocent and bold, she has many dreams and many ambitions in life to fulfill. She is eager, impatient, and enthusiastic. She is optimistic, generous, and kind. She'll no doubt have the fire sign temper, which she is wont to use sometimes to get her own way. Petulant, rebellious, and defiant, the fire Princess has all the verve and wherewithal to succeed in life—her optimism and her faith will take her far.

REVERSED

The reversed fire Princess, the Princess of Batons, is a bad-tempered, spoilt, selfish girl who thinks of no one but herself. She has to win and be number one. She likes to be the most outrageous and the center of attention at all times.

She is not content to be second best and is envious and jealous of any rivals. The reversed Princess must be taught that satisfying her own needs alone will never bring her the joy of selfless sharing or the bliss of an equal relationship. The reversed Princess may otherwise be left alone to revel in her fantasies in her ivory tower—locked up there so the rest of us can have some peace and quiet.

COINS: EARTH
(Taurus, Virgo, and Capricorn)

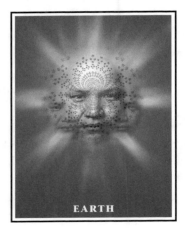

EARTH

King of Coins

The King of Coins, representing the earth signs, is an extremely capable, practical, and efficient person. He has an affinity with nature and a feel for design and form. He is a quiet and introverted man, gentle and shy. However, this should not mask his materialistic and ambitious nature, which is very powerful.

No one is better equipped to deal patiently with the long and slow climb to success than the King of Coins. He is a hard-working person who knows how to enjoy the fruits of his labors, and he has a sensuous appetite for many things. He may be a skilled worker and a dedicated team member. He is practical and down to earth, kind and compassionate, and sensible and practical to the end. He does not boast, squander, or waste. The King of Coins knows how to trim and conserve, and usually has something tucked away for a rainy day.

REVERSED

Stubborn, dull, downtrodden, greedy, miserly, and materialistic, the reversed King of Coins is a real stick in the mud. Always dissatisfied, he is so attuned to materialistic things that he finds no solace or pleasure elsewhere. In short, he has lost sight of the things of real value in his life.

EARTH

Queen of Coins

The Queen of Coins is a sensuous and caring woman. She is a home-lover, and a practical and sensible person. She is deliberate in speech and manner and somewhat cautious and introverted. She is also ambitious and considers social status and material possessions of great importance. She has healthy appetites and is sensual and earthy in all she does. She has an affinity with nature and a love of good food, and is well equipped either to fulfill her own ambitions, or marry someone of wealth and status who will do it for her. However, she can also be stubborn and narrow-minded. Like the King of Coins, she does best in a quiet and natural environment.

REVERSED

Grasping, materialistic, promiscuous, insensitive, brusque, and bullying, the reversed Queen of Coins is a hopeless social climber. She thinks only of material things and has lost sight of the things of real value in this life. Earth signs, of all the elements, are most bound to the Earth itself and the things of the Earth. For that reason, it is often hardest for them to reach upward to love and to the things of the spirit.

EARTH

Prince of Coins

Sensitive, quiet, and artistic, the Prince of Coins keeps his dreams to himself. He is sensible, down to earth, and keenly fond of nature and animals. He is a deeply loving person who has an affinity for nature and a quiet and deep understanding of the way things tick. Quietly ambitious, silent and deep, this young man will strive diligently and work hard for what he wants in life. Intelligent and practical, he is a sound friend and determined ally. He has an aptitude for business and finance and a healthy appetite for commercial success. He will work hard to achieve his goals.

REVERSED

Critical, stubborn, indifferent, depressive, and moody, the reversed Prince is a bitter and jealous youth who is not prepared to work for his rewards, but expects to receive them for nothing. He is lazy and so self-repressed that he doesn't know what he wants. The reversed prince would do well to attend to his diet because he is more sensitive than most to impurities and biochemical imbalances. Slow and unmotivated, he may need prodding.

EARTH

Princess of Coins

The Princess of Coins is down to earth, practical, sensible, levelheaded, and ambitious. She enjoys fine clothes and is artistic and creative. She has an affinity for nature and small furry animals, and is most in her element in green fields.

The princess of Coins is prepared to work slowly and patiently to get somewhere later in life. She should be encouraged to relax and enjoy herself in her youth, for underneath her calm exterior is a cautious and conservative soul who is so keyed up to do her best that her worst fear may be of failure. The Princess of Coins should be taught at an early age to strive for a healthy balance between work and play. Otherwise she will suffer later in life from neuroses that result from too much pressure on achievement in her earlier years.

REVERSED

Indifferent, moody, sarcastic, and unwilling, the reversed Princess of Coins has a mind of her own and is not afraid to use it. Stubborn, uncooperative, demanding, and impatient, she demands more and more. Economy is a key word for the reversed Princess. She should learn to distribute her energies more fairly and thoroughly in her life and to gain freedom from her material dependencies.

SWORDS: AIR
(Gemini, Libra, and Aquarius)

AIR

King of Swords

The King of Swords is an intellectual, intelligent, and independent person who dislikes restrictions or personal ties of any kind. He handles all issues in his life with an objective and logical approach. He is ambitious, rational, assertive, and highly analytical. He is always full of new ideas and inventions and capable of abstract thought, as he is not easily moved by emotional considerations. He has an affinity with literature, law, and the realm of ideas.

REVERSED

Selfish and aggressive, the reversed King of Swords can be cold, unemotional, cruel, and exacting in his dealings with others. All the bright ideas he could develop are restricted, either through lack of opportunity or because the ideas themselves are impractical. The reversed King lives by mind alone and has lost contact with his feelings, emotions, and spirituality. He sees only abstract logic and finds it hard to deal with issues that have an emotional or personal bias.

AIR

Queen of Swords

Intelligent, independent, and strong-willed, the Queen of Swords is a person who likes to explore the many options available to her. She is a career woman and an expert communicator, full of original and innovative ideas. She is curious and experimental, with a great appetite for facts and figures. Like her counterpart, the King of Swords, she is ideally suited to intellectual pursuits, literature, language, and law. She is more cerebral than emotional, and you can be sure that the Queen of Swords will filter everything carefully through her keen mind. Her thinking is quick and clear, and her unemotional bias enables her to be logical and astute in most areas of her life.

REVERSED

The reversed Queen of Swords is a cold, calculating woman who has no feelings for others, except for the experience and information they can impart to her. She is quite capable of separating her mind from her heart and therefore faces many emotional problems in her life. She is unable to feel love or emotion without the necessity to analyze and scrutinize them thoroughly. This can lead to emotional barrenness, loneliness, and feelings of isolation. The reversed Queen must be careful to practice what she preaches, as words, to her, have no more substance than the air with which they are spoken. The reversed Queen cannot experience love until she has learned to give it. Emotional isolation may be the result until she learns to acknowledge her own emotional needs and those of others.

Prince of Swords

The Prince of Swords is a bright, keen, enthusiastic and intelligent youth, capable of much study and achievement in the realm of abstract ideas. He may also be a good communicator and often has talent in the arts, particularly literature and drama, and an affinity with law. He can be dependent on others, in his youth, to supply or stimulate him with information on which to build his own logical structure. He will scrutinize every piece of data that comes his way until it fits neatly into his own scheme of things. He has an appetite for study and makes a capable student given the correct stimulus.

REVERSED

The reversed Prince of Swords scatters his energies and ideas at every whim or impulse. He is a crafty, calculating youth who will do anything to avoid responsibility. He is too busy exploring and experimenting, often in negative and detrimental areas, to achieve anything of substance. His ideas are impractical, and he is often misinformed. He is prone to mood swings; high elation followed by deep depression, as a result of negative and disconnected thinking. The reversed Prince desperately needs a clear view and much encouragement to get him back on a positive path. He must be encouraged to explore his own emotional needs as *de rigeur* (essential) for a healthy and whole existence. He tends to ignore both his own needs and those of others, dismissing them as "illogical."

AIR

Princess of Swords

The Princess of Swords is a perceptive, discerning, and vigilant youth. At all times she must filter her experiences through the logical framework upon which she is building her own philosophy.

She makes an excellent student and is quite capable of understanding the most abstract of ideas in an intellectual context. She excels in study and is often ambitious. She is drawn to media studies, the arts, business, and commerce. She is also inventive and intelligent. Given the right opportunities she has much to offer. She can be shy, often as an attempt to remain modest despite her many gifts and capabilities.

REVERSED

The reversed Princess is changeable, moody, demanding, crafty, and conceited at her own intellectual prowess, but emotionally cold and uncaring of others. The reversed Princess is a scandalous gossip and many friendships will be laid to waste by her overactive tongue. The reversed Princess will pay the price with emotional isolation if she does not acknowledge that her intellect is but one of the many functions of her own spirit.

CUPS: WATER
(Cancer, Scorpio, and Pisces)

WATER

King of Cups

The King of Cups, ruled as he is by water, is the most sensitive, psychic, and intuitive of the kings. Water, the greatest conductor of electrical energy, imparts a deep and silent aura of knowledge and wisdom to this suit. The King of Cups is emotional, secretive, and intense. His primary function is to experience everything exclusively through the realm of feeling and emotion. He is sentimental and easily hurt, and may relate better to women than men—women being more in tune with his sensitive nature. Due to his psychic and compassionate ways, the King of Cups makes an excellent alternative practitioner or counselor. He is also extremely astute. His impressions are not limited to his five senses, as he prefers to use his sixth sense. Tender and kind, but fiercely self-protective due to his sensitive nature, the King of Cups is a deep well of both wisdom and compassion.

REVERSED

The reversed King of Cups is a suspicious, jealous, self-pitying, and tyrannical man lost in a world of imagined hurts and slights. He is excessively emotional and lacks the cool logic that he needs to understand the myriad impressions he has already soaked up like a sponge. He is incapable of detachment in his thinking and everything takes on an emotional bias. The reversed King is lost, deep within himself, in the dark oceans of his own feelings. He needs to surface for air (logic).

WATER

Queen of Cups

The Queen of Cups is a compassionate and sensitive woman, deeply attuned to the emotional needs of others. She is psychic and intuitive, and her innate sixth sense tells her exactly what is happening in her environment. She is gentle, tender, and kindly, and easily empathizes with others. She is often artistic and is skilled at dealing with secrets and mysteries. She makes a good healer, counselor, nurse, teacher, or doctor and has a deep reservoir of emotional strength at her disposal. She is mysterious, shy, and deep, and does not share her personal feelings easily. As with all the water signs, the Queen of Cups must protect her own deep feelings first.

REVERSED

Illogical, irrational and overly emotional, the reversed Queen may be an addicted escapist or suffer serious neuroses due to her tendency to repress and deny her own feelings. She has no logical format by which to assess her life, and may be lost in her own paranoid world. She has soaked everything up like a sponge, including all the negative energies around her. The lifebelt she needs is one of logical and practical solutions to her own emotional dilemmas.

WATER

Prince of Cups

Quiet, sensitive, and shy, the Prince of Cups is a deeply impressionable youth who is gentle and kind. He needs much affection and will find security in a loving environment that can cater to his emotional needs and where he, too, can give of himself emotionally. He is fond of animals and children, and is a warm and tender person. He is not an intellectual in the normal sense of the word, and prefers studies or occupations that allow him to use his greater gifts—those of intense depth of feeling, psychic sensitivity, and the vivid imagination shared by all the water signs.

REVERSED

The reversed Prince of Cups, especially if he is a Scorpio, will be cruel, vengeful, suspicious, and trusting of no one. He is lost in his own imagination and feelings. Paranoid, deluded, and obsessive, he is totally out of touch not only with others but with himself as well.

He is a bully, emotionally demanding, and self-centered. His only wish is that his emotional needs are met. The reversed Prince is incapable of logical thought and is trapped in an emotionally confused world of his own making.

WATER

Princess of Cups

Tender, emotional, and compassionate, the Princess of Cups is a sensitive and aware youth who often keeps her feelings to herself. She is very responsive and receptive to the needs of others and kind with animals and children. She may find it hard to deal with the demands of her family or society generally, as she spends much time in a world of her own imagination. She may have artistic and acting ability, being sensitive to the vibrations of others, or find a calling in the caring professions of nursing, healing, and teaching. Given the right nurturing environment, this normally quiet and shy girl can achieve much with her innate inner wisdom.

REVERSED

Self-centered, highly emotional, and willful, the reversed Princess of Cups is never satisfied or fulfilled unless her own emotional needs are being met. She is interested in no one's feelings but her own and may demand much attention at all times. She may draw attention to herself by creating various emotional dramas, but is rarely satisfied. Balancing out highly charged emotions with a more logical and practical approach may be essential to her ultimate nature and well-being.

PART THREE

PREPARING FOR READINGS

The One World deck does not necessarily have to be wrapped in silk or hidden away, but it should be kept in an appropriate place and treated with respect at all times. You should not keep your cards near electrical equipment or near any object with negative vibrations or connotations.

If you are traveling with your deck, it will be quite happy as it is, in your bag, or briefcase, without special treatment. But as I have said, it is only right that the tarot deck, so full of knowledge, should be treated with respect and handled carefully and gently at all times.

For reading the cards, I find it best to locate a suitable space within my home or office. This place should be quiet, clean, and fresh. I then make a sacred space within that area, either by visualizing a bubble of light that will encase, protect, and encourage a healing vibration, or by visualizing a pyramid that will encompass the space where I am working. I also like to adorn this space with fresh flowers, candles, and incense and may also have some soft new age music playing.

The area should be an uplifting, safe, and trusting one in which free energy and communication can take place between reader and querent. A free flow of thought and vibration stimulates a healthy atmosphere in which both reader and querent can relax and tune in.

I believe it is absolutely essential that the reader is clean, fresh, calm, and concentrated on the job at hand. The mind of the reader must be clear and focused solely on tuning in to the querent. Relaxation or concentration techniques before the reading can help. Spend time before a reading with a clear mind focused exclusively on the reading. If you do several readings in a row, you can boost your energy between readings by deep breathing and relaxation techniques.

When the querent arrives for their reading, they should be shown into the reading area and made welcome and comfortable. You can spend ten minutes or so beforehand just warming up with them, perhaps having an informal chat in the meantime, or offering them a cup of herb tea.

Remove the cards from their resting place and place them on the table. Ask the querent to shuffle the cards, in his or her own time, and to concentrate on the questions he or she may have.

If you are working with a spirit guide, take a few moments to silently tune into them and kindly ask for their help. If possible, acknowledge the querent's guide, even if you can't see them, so that both may help you give the correct information or advice. It is a small gesture, but one that, I feel, goes a long way.

THE ASTROLOGICAL SPREAD

The Astrological Spread comprises twelve cards laid out in circular motion starting from the left and working counterclockwise, with one extra card placed in the middle of the circle.

The twelve positions are related to the astrological houses through which the planetary and zodiacal powers manifest onto the Earth plane, and which describe the main archetypal divisions of our lives.

Each position has an affinity with the astrological house that details an aspect of the querent's life. The twelve primary positions may be described thus:

FIRST HOUSE

NATURAL RULER: ARIES
PLANETARY RULER: MARS

The First House describes how the querent is feeling about him or herself and how he or she is projecting oneself to others. It may also refer to beginnings, or the querent's early life and childhood.

SECOND HOUSE

NATURAL RULER: TAURUS
PLANETARY RULER: VENUS

The Second House describes the querent's material possessions, home, and financial position. It may also detail ways in which the querent can or will earn a living, or the location at which he or she may choose to live or work.

THIRD HOUSE

NATURAL RULER: GEMINI
PLANETARY RULER: MERCURY

The Third House describes how the querent is interacting with friends, neighbors, and siblings. It can also indicate short journeys, journeys by air, or journeys to countries with a third-house connection (for example, USA or Wales).

FOURTH HOUSE

NATURAL RULER: CANCER
PLANETARY RULER: MOON

The Fourth House describes the emotional state of the querent and has direct reference to the emotional relationships with family members and the mother in particular.

FIFTH HOUSE

NATURAL RULER: LEO
PLANETARY RULER: SUN

The Fifth House describes the creativity of the querent and his or her love affairs. It has an affinity with the arts and theater.

SIXTH HOUSE

NATURAL RULER: VIRGO
PLANETARY RULER: MERCURY

The Sixth House describes the health of the querent and his or her work potential.

SEVENTH HOUSE

NATURAL RULER: LIBRA
PLANETARY RULER: VENUS

The Seventh House defines business partnerships and marriage.

EIGHTH HOUSE

NATURAL RULER: SCORPIO
PLANETARY RULERS: MARS AND PLUTO

The Eighth House relates to other people's money, the unconscious, death, legacy and inheritance. It also describes the sexual nature of the querent.

NINTH HOUSE

NATURAL RULER: SAGITTARIUS
PLANETARY RULER: JUPITER

The Ninth House describes long-distance journeys, education and expansion, religious and philosophical attitudes.

TENTH HOUSE

NATURAL RULER: CAPRICORN
PLANETARY RULER: SATURN

The Tenth House describes the career potential and the status of the querent.

ELEVENTH HOUSE

NATURAL RULER: AQUARIUS
PLANETARY RULER: URANUS

The Eleventh House details groups and social events connected to the querent, and also indicates that which is sudden or unexpected.

TWELFTH HOUSE

NATURAL RULER: PISCES
PLANETARY RULERS: JUPITER AND NEPTUNE

The Twelfth House relates to institutions, hospitals, art, imagination, secret friends or enemies, and romantic affairs.

THE THIRTEENTH CARD

This card, although it is laid out last, connects the beginning and the end of the reading. It is the central card with the primary message of the whole reading.

Should you or the querent have need of more detail, you may proceed to lay out twelve additional cards on the outside of the original twelve.

INTERPRETATIONS

The tarot, like other forms of divination, acts as a focus, or a springboard, from where the subconscious (superconscious) mind can operate.

The symbolic images of the tarot stimulate the intuition. With continued practice your psychic powers will develop slowly but surely. Indeed, they may develop to a point at which a mere glance at a card will allow the symbolism to reach the unconscious and activate the intuitive powers of the mind.

Most people who use the tarot use it precisely because it is an intuitive system with no necessity to study the theory behind it. Like most things, however, the deeper our understanding, the deeper our knowledge and the more expert we become in understanding the prime factors composing our lives and the meanings of our lives as reflected in the tarot images.

Each card has many meanings and each position of the cards also has several interpretations. It is up to the reader, through skill and mastery of the subject and through sensitive appraisal of the querent, to apply the correct interpretation in each case.

Now that you have familiarized yourself with the meanings of the cards themselves, and memorized the significance of the position of the cards in the Astrological Spread, it is simply a question of putting two and two together. As each card and each position have meanings of their own, they must be combined with the knowledge of the query, so that an interpretation can be made.

To illustrate, let us investigate one of the Major Arcana in each of the twelve positions. This will show how the interpretation would vary, position-to-position, dependent on the query.

Let us look then, at the High Priest, ruled by Jupiter, which is known to bring luck, expansion, travel, and so on.

V The High Priest in the First House

The querent is an expansive, honest, and philosophical individual who is currently in a good position to expand his/her personal potential. The querent will be fortunate and popular. Travel or spiritual studies may enhance this development further. The querent is trustworthy and kind and makes an excellent friend. The querent also has good powers of perception and imagination, is sociable and extroverted, and has a warm and genuine personality.

V The High Priest in the Second House

If the querent has any problems regarding finances or property, he/she can be assured that his/her transactions will be very fortunate and financially advantageous. As the High Priest is ruled by Jupiter and has connections with long-distance travel and foreign people or places, the querent may be fortunate in acquiring money and/or property overseas, or may find fortune abroad.

V The High Priest in the Third House

The querent has excellent communication skills that should be developed. He or she makes a good teacher, lecturer, singer, writer, etc. Good news may be on the way, with the possibility of overseas communications, travel, air journeys (usually long distance). As the USA is a Gemini country, this position has relevance to travel to or within the States or may indicate many short-distance journeys. As Gemini is also connected to brothers, sisters, and neighbors, the High Priest in the Third House may indicate good news or good fortune for or from those people, dependent on the query.

V The High Priest in the Fourth House

The querent is kind, generous and emotionally warm. He or she will benefit through the family and, with the Fourth House connection to Cancer, the home and mother in particular. If the question relates to the querent's mother, this card indicates good fortune and success, provided, of course, it is not reversed.

V The High Priest in the Fifth House

The querent will be very fortunate in creative endeavors, and love affairs will be well-starred. This card in this position may also relate to love affairs with a Jovian influence, or love affairs while in foreign countries. It may also indicate talent in the performing arts, and that the querent will do well in his/her profession during journeys abroad.

V The High Priest in the Sixth House

As the Sixth House governs service to others and health this card here is an indication that the querent will do well in his/her profession. With an affinity for teaching, healing, and hygiene, the querent may expect benefits in those areas. If the query is about health, Jupiter's rulership of this card would indicate liverishness, sluggishness, hip, or thigh problems, nervousness, restlessness, and sleeplessness. However, it also promises good health to come if the querent takes the appropriate action to remedy his/her malady. Beneficial plants and remedies for Sagittarius and/or liver complaints are dandelion, sage, liverwort, and vervain.

V The High Priest in the Seventh House

This card in this position promises great good fortune through marriage or partnership. It may also indicate partnership with someone foreign or marriage to a foreigner. Alternatively, the marriage (business) partner may be Sagittarian or Piscean (Jupiter rules both) or a successful and confident person (Jupiter). It may also indicate success in legal matters if the query is of a legal nature, as the Seventh House is ruled by Libra, which has an affinity with marriage, partnership, and the law. This position has connections with Venus, and if the question is of a career nature, it may indicate success in the arts.

V The High Priest in the Eighth House

The High Priest in this position may indicate financial gain through inheritance, speculation, or tax returns. It may also indicate sexual attraction to someone of a foreign nationality or general good fortune in those areas.

V The High Priest in the Ninth House

The High Priest in this position indicates the possibilities of long-distance travel (possibly to Australia, as Australia is ruled by Sagittarius), or to other countries ruled by this sign. The querent is generally fortunate and expansive. Success in educational matters is indicated, acceptance at university, success with exams, and so on. Foreign travel is well-starred, and success may be had in foreign lands.

V The High Priest in the Tenth House

Ruling the career and status of the querent as it does, this card promises great career success, with the querent rising to the top of his/her profession. He or she is honest, trustworthy, and imaginative, and rules with both wisdom and vision. Career success may be experienced in the areas governed by Jupiter, or countries ruled by same.

V The High Priest in the Eleventh House

Changes may be very sudden and unexpected when this card appears here, but will be to the querent's advantage. The querent may find good fortune in the areas ruled by Aquarius, such as technology, computers, and television. Clubs, groups, and societies will also be of benefit to the querent, either in a spiritual capacity (yoga, meditation, etc.) or in terms of mental interest, through travel clubs or night classes.

V The High Priest in the Twelfth House

The querent has wonderful vision, intuition and imagination, and may find benefit in these areas. As the Twelfth House rules hospitals and institutions, if the question is of a career nature, the querent will find success and benefit in these areas. The card may indicate journeys overseas with a Twelfth House/Pisces connection.

V The High Priest as the central card

The central card takes on the central meaning of the reading. The High Priest here is very auspicious for the core message. Expansive, fortunate, and promising good fortune, this card indicates that the querent is in a position to expand his/her life, potential and personality.

The cards, the position of the cards, and the querent's questions all affect the interpretation of the cards. Although it may at first seem a little hard on the memory cells, it won't be long before you feel at home with your readings, and confident in your understanding and interpretations.

Read always with love and respect, carefully consider and phrase your interpretations, and respect your clients' confidentiality.

Good luck with your readings!

APPLICATIONS

Over the last twenty years or so, we have seen a rapid development and increasing popularity of all forms of therapy, counseling, and healing, which now seem to be merging into one all-embracing holistic system.

The holistic system of healing (holistic means to "make whole") is based on the understanding that human beings are not purely material or physical forms, and that illness is a direct reflection of imbalances in the psyche. The imbalances in the psyche can be seen as part of individual evolutionary process toward perfect balance, wholeness and completion, which Jung described as individuation.

The imbalances result from individual belief systems and behavior patterns and personal perception of one's place in the universal scheme of things. The impressions imprinted on the personal psyche are a net result of the individual's response to the ongoing process of self-development. The personal belief system one builds up around oneself is an attempt to maintain one's own persona, sense of individuality, or mask.

While we attempt to maintain our individual masks, the inner psyche is not only little understood but is rarely even addressed. In *Life and the Realization of the Self*, psychotherapist Eduardo Pitchon writes, "Psychotherapy has a holy function, namely, the ancient and sacred function of healing. In psychotherapy we attempt to help a person to come back to himself and we encourage the development of a more mature relation between a person and his inner core. We all have an inner world and we all live in that world. The inner world is all that exists for us. It is all we know, all that we have experienced and all that we will ever know or ever experience. The inner world and the outer world are one and the same thing because there is only one world. The problem lies in the fact that we are not aware of it. The inner world encompasses everything, whether we are aware of it or not, and it is beyond the limits of time and space."

The purpose of the tarot in psychology, counseling, and healing is to illuminate the invisible aspects of the self through a process of self-reflection and inquiry. The process will point the patient/client to the hidden aspects of his or her own psyche. A process of healing is enabled through self-awareness.

The causative factors in any imbalance, whether physical, emotional, or mental, are rooted deep within the individual psyche. For any true healing to occur, the root of the problem must be illuminated, addressed, and remedied.

Tarot cards have been used over the centuries primarily as a form of divination, or "fortune-telling." The One World deck, with its astrological information and specific archetypal allocations, makes it possible to use the tarot for other applications.

The One World deck is a useful tool for psychoanalysis and counseling, as it can be used intuitively and symbolically to define aspects of the psyche that need reviewing. A little study will open it as an effective guide and tool to reflect unseen aspects of our own or our client's natures.

Should you wish to employ this deck in therapy or counseling, ask your client or patient to think about his or her problems and to shuffle the cards for the analyst or reader to interpret. In this way, the unconscious (super-conscious) of the client is brought to the surface in a very short space of time. Due to the abstract and symbolic nature of the visuals in the One World deck, both client and therapist may enjoy a new dimension in counseling.

Our physical well-being is linked inexorably to our mental and spiritual well-being. When we heal the spirit, we heal the mind-when we heal the mind, we heal the body. The use of the One World deck in assisting the healing process is invaluable. The whole reading will give an accurate assessment of the querent's state of physical and mental health. Diagnosis of any particular health problem will be highlighted through the card in the sixth house position.

Practitioners of psychology and healers within the counseling fields can use the One World deck as a means of enabling the client or patient to express aspects of their personality through the symbolism of the tarot cards.

Alternatively, the One World deck can be utilized for meditation and visualization. For instance, to improve

mental faculties and communication skills, or to emphasize a particular energy or attribute, you can meditate
(focus) on the card that best conveys the energy you
need to stimulate. The Magician, for instance, would
help communication skills, students, and writers. (I personally kept a framed copy of The Magician on my desk
throughout the writing of this book as a tool to help keep
my intellectual faculties rolling and to facilitate a flow
between my left and right brain.) Should you need added
confidence, try meditating on the Sun card. If you need
a little luck, focus on the healing energies of the High
Priest, and so on.

Color therapy and symbolism work through the colors on the cards and can stimulate various organs and
energies within you. You can meditate with your eyes
open or shut on the various cards of the One World deck,
as color is an actual vibration that you perceive at a deep
level regardless of vision. However, when you meditate
with your eyes open on some of the One World deck
images, you will actually start to see them move.
Although there was no intention in the design process to
give optical effects to the cards, they have evolved
nonetheless. For example, if you stare at the Sun card
you will start to see it rotate. The World and the
Magician, too, will spin for you. The Buddha will float
and the Fool will twinkle around the heavens. All you
have to do is to keep focusing, albeit in a relaxed way on
the image itself, for a few minutes.

However you choose to employ your One World deck, whether it be for divination, healing, psychology, counseling or meditation, I, again, and for the last time in this book, wish you all the very best of luck and hope you enjoy working with your deck.

—Crystal Love

London, 5 July 2002.

BIBLIOGRAPHY

Brown, Dee. *Bury My Heart at Wounded Knee: An Indian History of the American West.* New York: Henry Holt & Company, Inc., 1991.

Dee, Nerys. *Your Dreams and What They Mean: The Secret Language of Sleep.* U.K.: Aquarian Press, 1984.

Dunne, J.W. *An Experiment with Time.* New York: Hampton Roads Publishing Company, Inc., 2001.

Cockell, Jenny. *Across Time and Death: A Mother's Search for Her Past Life Children.* New York: Simon & Schuster, 1994.

Levi, Eliphas. *Le Dogme et Rituel de la Haute Magie.* Paris: 1854.

Mitchell, PhD, Robert Cameron. *African Primal Religions.* Illinois: Argus Communications, 1977.

Pitchon, Eduardo. "Life and the Realization of the Self." (manuscript)

Rose, Colin Penfield. *Accelerated Learning.* New York: Dell Publishing Company, Inc., 1987.

Rudgely, Richard. *The Encyclopedia of Psycho-active Substances.* New York: St. Martin's Press, 2000.

Sepharial. *The Manual of Astrology.* New Mexico: Sun Publishing Company, 1981.

Sepharial. *Hebrew Astrology.* New Mexico: Sun Publishing Company, 1981.

Starck, Marcia. *Healing with Astrology.* California: Crossing Press, 1997.

Tompkins, Peter and Bird, Christopher. *The Secret Life of Plants.* New York: HarperTrade, 1989.

Wilson, Colin. *Alien Dawn.* New York: International Publishing Corporation, 1998.

SPECIAL ACKNOWLEDGMENTS

I am indebted to the following scholarly works which have contributed much knowledge to this project, and from which certain passages are quoted.

Alien Dawn, by Colin Wilson. New York: International Publishing Corporation, 1998.

Tarot Classic, by Stuart Kaplan. Stamford, CT: U.S. Games Systems, Inc., 1972.

An Experiment with Time, by J.W. Dunne. New York: Hampton Roads Publishing Company, Inc., 2001.

How to Foretell Your Future in the Cards, by Kathleen McCormack. U.K.: Fontana Books, 1973.

Jung and the Tarot, by Sallie Nichols. York Beach, ME: Samuel Weiser Inc., 1980.

Mastering the Tarot, by Eden Gray. New York: Signet, 1971.

The Tarot: A Key to the Wisdom of the Ages, by Paul Foster Case. Richmond, VA: Macoy Publishing Co., 1947.

The Tarot, by Alfred Douglas. U.K.: Gollancz & Co., 1973.

Tarot: Path to Self Development, by Michelene Stuart. U.S.A: Shambhala Publications, Inc., 1995.

Tarot: The Royal Path to Wisdom, by Joseph D'Agostino. York Beach, ME: Samuel Weiser Inc., 1976.

The Tarot Speaks, by Richard Gardner. U.K.: Rigel Press, 1971.

Understanding the Tarot: A Practical Guide to Tarot Card Reading, by Jocelyn Almond and Keith Seddon. U.K.: Aquarian, 1992.

ABOUT THE AUTHOR/CREATOR

Crystal Love (Sagittarius) is an astrologer, psychic, and healer who has appeared extensively on UK radio and television discussing the mystical and supernatural.

Her first book to be published, *The Mystic Mind* (Fusion Press, London 2000) uses a plethora of case histories, hard data, factual, and scientific evidence to prove such phenomena as telepathy, soul projection, life after death, and reincarnation to be logical realities.

She currently lives in London and is also a ceramic sculptor and painter with a keen interest in music and the visual arts in general.

ABOUT THE ARTIST

Michael Hobbs (Virgo) is a successful computer graphics designer and digital artist with an early history in film advertising. His current projects have a mainly musical, ecological, or humanitarian bias.

Michael is also an avid traveler and has spent time exploring in Europe, India, Nepal, Mexico, Australia, New Zealand, and the Far East.

He is also a talented musician and photographer with many interests ranging from football to philosophy.